LEADING FOR PERFORMANCE

Inspire • Motivate • Engage

7 Principles for Leading
Highly Effective Teams

Oliver Wright

Fisher King Publishing

LEADING FOR PERFORMANCE

Copyright © Oliver Wright 2023

Print ISBN 978-1-914560-76-7
Digital ISBN 978-1-914560-77-4

Published by Fisher King Publishing
fisherkingpublishing.co.uk

"People… need to know what the plan of action is and how it will be implemented. They want to be given responsibility to help solve the problem and the authority to act on it."

Howard Schultz

Contents

INTRODUCTION

"Always treat your employees exactly as
you want them to treat your
best customers."

Stephen R. Covey

The purpose of this book is to help managers and leaders to appreciate, understand and apply the key principles and practices that will enable them to become better leaders and build better teams. To create happier and more engaged people that work together to deliver improved performance.

My aim is to provide practical, straightforward ways of applying the lessons so that you have a how to guide you can use in your organisation and with your team.

It is founded on the belief that leaders perform best when they get out of the way and resist trying to manage and control everything, but instead inspire, motivate, enable, champion, and support.

It comes from the perspective of someone who has worked in a leadership role, has studied leadership theory, and practiced coaching. I am offering knowledge for real world application that will enable leaders (new and experienced) to put the learnings into practice in their organisations.

It pulls together a number of strands and principles into a coherent whole, where all the parts work together and there is a logic to how the pieces fit together. Many other texts focus on one piece of the puzzle but do not offer the working leader a complete picture of how the interlinking and interdependent parts fit together to drive real change and impact performance.

The book looks to cover all aspects of the leader's real-world

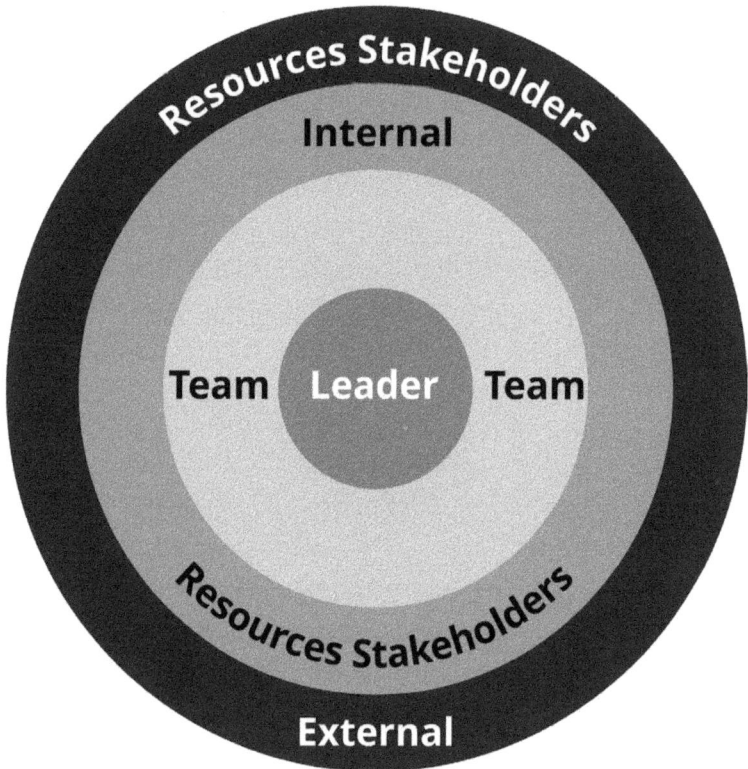

predicament and all the critical success factors:

- Team and team dynamics.
- The importance of the leader and their behaviours.
- Performance critical relationships with internal and external stakeholders (including customers).
- Access to resources within the team and outside of the team, without which success is not possible.

7 Principles for Leading Highly Effective Teams

Focusing on 7 principles it aims to help you become a more inspirational and effective leader who gets out of the way and enables your team to succeed.

1. It Starts with You
2. Shared Purpose
3. Direction and Decision Making
4. Delegate and Empower
5. Coach for Performance
6. Emotional Safety
7. Provide, Protect and Champion

The book provides practical, tried, and tested ways to become a better leader and build better teams. I break things down into actionable steps that you can implement in the real world.

Learn how to create a self-managed, highly motivated, and creative team that innovates and delivers results. Create more motivated and engaged employees and help reduce stress in the workplace to maximise the potential of your people. Free up your time as a leader to support and champion your team and focus on your strategic priorities.

Use your time to keep learning and focusing on continual improvement, remaining agile. Supporting and championing your team and securing the resources you and your team need to be successful.

I focus on the unit of a team because the majority of leaders are leading teams, however large and complex those teams may be.

In the end a great leader is a great team leader who people want to follow and to support. Teams are the key cogs in the engine of the organisation, if each team is led well then, the organisation works. Exceptional individuals can make a difference, but as you will discover in this book, it's not individuals that drive high performance it is teams.

In essence the book is focused on bringing about behavioural and cultural change by building a highly effective behavioural skill set in the leader and the team. One of the biggest mistakes leaders and managers can make (including myself) when trying to elicit or encourage behavioural change is to talk in generalities that the individual can do nothing with. For example, "you need to have more impact", "you need to delegate more", "you need to be more visionary". This causes the person to leave the meeting thinking, "Yeah well, I know I need be all those things, but this has got me no further along the path to doing it! How do I do it?"

I am providing guidance, ideas, and inspiration on "how to" that I believe are useful and practical things that will deliver real value and have real world impact in your team and organisation. They will move you towards the leadership behaviours that build learning, high performing, creative teams that will beat their competition.

I am going to cover some practical advice and guidance on delegating and empowering, how to establish a shared purpose. How to work on developing a growth mindset and feeling secure in yourself, how to encourage open communication and emotional safety within the team. As well as how to use coaching as a leader, which is fundamental to achieving this goal. And finally looking at the importance of, and how to support and champion your team to protect them and secure the resources they need.

I don't believe this is the easiest or most comfortable way to lead but I do believe it is the most effective approach for many leadership situations. Like everything in life that delivers real value and satisfaction it takes effort, commitment, and bravery.

You may be a new leader, or you may have developed a number of these skills already, and perhaps you want to just dip into those areas that are underdeveloped or new to you. I want you to be able to jump to any section of the book based on what you need.

Whatever stage you feel you are at I hope you find something useful you can apply to make you an even better leader.

1. Changing the Way Leaders Behave

"Happy employees ensure happy customers. And happy customers ensure happy shareholders - in that order."

Simon Sinek

The Empowering Leader

As I'm sure most would agree, business leaders need to be driven to succeed (but not at all costs), to be results focused, and be able to make decisions. They should ensure that their team performs to the best of its ability and delivers its objectives. A leader cannot be successful without their team or people succeeding.

How you do this, is what I believe makes the biggest difference to delivering long term sustainable performance and competitive advantage from motivated and engaged employees.

Leadership should be about unlocking and maximising people's potential by creating an environment where they share a sense of purpose, feel empowered to be creative and make decisions, learn from their mistakes and from each other, and feel motivated to continually improve.

The best leaders are open, self-aware, confident enough to listen to all voices, to embrace change, provide clear direction and make the big decisions at the right time. They have a growth and learning mindset, care about their employees and build relationships based on respect.

To be successful leaders need to build motivated, self-managed teams with the ability to get things done, and then get out of the way. The best leaders let their workers work, leaving them to get on with it and to do what they do best.

3M are one of the most innovative companies in the world, known for Post-It notes, Scotch tape, and other inventions. William Coyne headed their research and development for over a decade. He espoused the view that through his experience as a researcher he knew that leaving teams to get on with it and limiting executive interference generated more creativity and better results. When he became head of R&D, he was determined to get out of the way and allow his teams to work for periods of time without interference. Coyne limited executive interference and managed his own involvement because, as he said, "After you plant a seed in the ground, you don't dig it up every week to see how it is doing."

This kind of leadership is not easy, but it is the best way to maximise engagement, motivation and to unlock the maximum potential from your people.

What this style of leadership is NOT advocating is that the leader stops providing leadership, and just becomes part of the team. The leader still has a clear and distinct role to play and is ultimately accountable for the performance of their team, as will become clear throughout this book. I am also not advocating that leaders are absolved from making the tough decisions required to be successful or to protect the business in the long term. Leaders have to provide clear direction, instil a strong behavioural code of conduct and be clear about expectations on compliance and ethics.

Leaders should be explicit about what they expect, they are the ones who are accountable for making the big decisions and for the consequences of those decisions. But it's the way they do it that can be different.

I see it as the intersection of a number of key behavioural skills in three areas of Drive, Self, and Team that combined make a successful leader who can maximise the engagement, motivation, and potential of their team.

Self
Self Aware
Growth Mindset

Empowering Leadership

Drive
Shared Purpose
Direction & Decisive
Effective Delegation

Team
Coach & Develop
Emotional Safety
Champion & Protect

Self is about the notion that it starts with you. As a leader you take on additional responsibility, not just in organisation terms, but also for your team. You can no longer just be the same person you were before you were a leader because you now have a responsibility to look after, develop and motivate your team to give their best and to help them reach their full potential.

Increasing your self-awareness is the starting point. We need to hold a mirror up to ourselves and seek feedback from others so that we can be consciously aware of our behaviour and its impact on others. We should become aware, as leaders, of the behaviours we need to stop, modify, and start to be the most effective leader we can be. Adopting a growth mindset helps us act positively to feedback and implement change in the spirit of continual improvement and development.

Drive is about the all-important need for leaders to develop and maintain forward momentum to implement their strategies to drive performance by focusing on delivering results in all areas. Forward momentum is critical in any aspect of business. Delivering small changes, small wins or incremental growth can help increase confidence and gives a foundation to build upon. Success is built step by step, so driving people and the team to take the first step and celebrate the progress made is a great way to build confidence and momentum. The way leaders do this is by developing a shared purpose with their people, giving clear direction, setting clear goals, ensuring buy-in and ownership of goals and then empowering people to deliver through effective delegation.

Team is about recognising that as a leader your team is the engine that will drive results. People should be the focus of your energies so that you can maximise the potential of each team member through the high-performance learning culture that you create with your team.

It is not always possible to get all of these things right and no one is going to be perfect at everything, but it is definitely worth focusing on achieving a balance across the three areas. Simply focusing on Drive, for example, will help you improve performance but without focusing on the other areas you will not maximise the benefits gained, and it may not be as sustainable a performance benefit.

You will note from the 7 principles that the order is Self, Drive and Team. Even though you will probably be working on all areas concurrently. There is a logic to the order. Firstly, if you do not start with yourself, you will not be able to successfully deliver on the other parts of the model, which are dependent on you having a strong sense of self, and an openness to feedback and change. The Drive components are all first order leadership behaviours; skills and techniques that set you and your team up for success they provide a framework for building a high performing self-managed team.

The so called "soft skills" involved are not soft in their effect. They are very powerful because they build engagement and motivation, which delivers direct benefits to the organisation through increased discretionary effort, less time spent on internal politics and greater innovation through continual learning.

Achieving a level of competency in all of these areas and then balancing the different areas to ensure forward momentum and continual improvement will deliver improved performance.

Why Leaders Need to Change

There is still a tendency for many organisations to be hierarchical, rule based and bureaucratic with hierarchical interactions based on task accomplishment, reward, and punishment, rather than meaningful relationships, two-way dialogue, and genuine collaboration. This results in a traditional leader-follower power dynamic. (Schein and Schein 2018)

Schein and Schein found that the most common style of leadership in organisations is still largely transactional. One of control, whereby leaders seek to build individual power. Organisations typically reward individual performance - they put a premium on individual delivery in the short term to hit annual, quarterly, or monthly targets for key stakeholders i.e., the board and, or shareholders.

This model is not fit for purpose for the modern organisation and is completely at odds with the type of leadership necessary to create high performing teams, which in turn create high performing organisations that deliver results.

Schein and Schein (2018) argue that current managerial culture derived from this transactional, leader-follower model is myopic and has blind spots because of a lack of feedback and challenge.

Many organisations have also become increasingly complex as they put in more layers of control, bureaucracy, and reporting lines to try and control how things get done. This adds to the already high-level of task complexity and rate of change that is now the norm for most organisations. Complexity rarely, if ever, makes things more efficient, or creative or agile, in fact it can stifle innovation and reduce responsiveness.

A survey of leaders looking at the future of organisations and leadership found that there will be an increasing requirement for leaders and organisations to change the way they work if they are going to be competitive in the future. They note that organisations will need to break down obstacles and processes which have traditionally slowed down transformation and look at how they are organised. "Structure can cause additional red tape and slow the ability to change direction. Having less structure allows ideas to be easily adapted to the changing environment." (Grant Thornton Global, 2022)

You can't have less structure successfully without having self-managed learning teams, who are capable and supported properly to get on with things and make decisions in a more efficient and agile way than the previous hierarchical management structure.

The same study also found that whilst there will still be a need for leaders of dynamic organisations to have a clear vision and be able to articulate it, they "...need to understand that they don't have to have all the answers – but do need to ask the right questions and have a team surrounding them who are just as passionate about the vision as they are." (Grant Thornton Global, 2022)

The Blame Game

A consequence of the traditional top down, transactional structure and culture highlighted above is that it almost inevitably leads to the 'blame game', where individuals look to avoid being linked to mistakes or failures because reward and power is based on individual performance, not collective responsibility.

Blame and recrimination undermine morale, reduce

engagement, and unfortunately lead to a failure to fix what needs fixing. Focusing on blame only leads to others not wanting to come forward, it leads to mistakes and failures being hidden and most crucially for long term success, a failure to learn. This can mean high employee turnover and missed opportunities for innovation and increased revenue. In safety dependent industries however, lives can even be put at risk. "When people are afraid to speak up, bad things happen." (Hood 2015).

A tragic example is the dramatic change in culture at Boeing in the late 1990s when it merged with Lockheed Martin. Historically Boeing was an engineering led company with a focus on quality first and profit second. It had a strong learning culture which meant that people could point out when things weren't working and when mistakes were made without fear of retribution or humiliation. This all changed post-merger with a shift to focus on shareholder value that meant cost and speed to market not engineering excellence became the watchword. This also changed the culture to one of blame and fear, with engineers and workers being demoted, humiliated, and even fired for pointing out safety concerns, mistakes, and quality issues. The result was the 737 Max being allowed to fly and resulting in two fatal accidents and the death of hundreds of innocent people. (Downfall: The Case Against Boeing, 2021)

The Learning Organisation

Failure to learn is the biggest loss to an organisation's success and to the development of people and culture.

In order to compete and win in the coming decades, organisations need to become learning organisations. People, organisations, and teams should be winning or learning. Learning from everything that is happening within the organisation, both good and bad, from competitors, and other industries. Continual learning should be built into the processes, language, behaviour, and culture of the organisation.

A positive example of a company becoming a learning organisation and reaping the benefits is WD40. I'm sure you know the brand and probably have a blue and yellow can at home somewhere, but you don't necessarily think about the company that produces it. The company has undergone some major changes since the late 1990s, moving from a highly profitable one product company, with the vast majority of its sales from the US market, to become a multiproduct global company within ten years. This was a major strategic shift and to be successful they built a learning organisation, requiring employees to ask questions, to innovate, collaborate with each other, take risks and not be afraid of failure. The company went from turnover of $130 million to over $450m today and it is still highly profitable.

The amount of disruption that companies face is already high and will increase, with the advent of advanced artificial intelligence influencing not only how people work but also whether their jobs continue to exist. This is set against a backdrop of the reshaping of globalisation, shifts in geo-economic and political power, and changes in population across the world. All this means that companies will need to constantly innovate, evolve, and improve. To do this successfully they need an engaged workforce and a learning culture. One that supports learning, change and innovation so continual improvement becomes the norm, and step change innovation has the chance to emerge and be acted upon.

There is little argument, in theory at least, about the importance of innovation, continual improvement and marginal gains, but these things are impossible without continual learning.

Leaders will be required to internalise and understand the link between learning, continual improvement, and innovation. If they can make this connection, they can join the dots and realise that you can't build a learning organisation without an open culture that empowers people and supports open communication so that people can talk about mistakes and failures without fear of retribution, so that things can be learned.

In such an environment, the ability to engage staff and persuade them to follow a new vision will be essential. There is a need for leaders to be honest and direct. The traditional organisational structure, culture, and leadership style needs to adapt.

Organisations must ask if they have fully embraced the role of the leader who, coaches and empowers their team, gets out of the way so they can do their job, whilst providing support, direction, and decisiveness?

This kind of leader is successful when the team is successful, and gains influence and power through their team's performance.

Employees Want Change

"Companies that execute with purpose are more likely to generate long-term value. And people expect business to do more than make money for shareholders." (McKinsey, 2022)

Employees are pushing for change in the way organisations operate and how power dynamics work. We see survey after survey of employees, particularly millennials and Gen Z's showing what people want from work is not to be controlled or to act like a robot. All employees, whatever generation, want to be treated with respect. They want to be listened to, to achieve work-life balance and to do meaningful work that plays a role in strategic goals and, ideally, in society. The Gen Z's and millennials are bringing it to the fore because they have a different outlook on life and are more willing to be vocal about their expectations than previous generations, particularly post Covid.

Employees want to work at places that have a sense of purpose - and may leave if they don't find it.

The quiet quitting phenomena of 2021/22 is just another startling indication that many people, as much as half of the workforce, according to a recent Gallup survey, are disengaged, dissatisfied, and disinclined to do more than the bare minimum for their boss.

Gallup surveyed 15,000 Americans in June 2022 and found that the proportion of engaged employees in the US workforce dropped to a six-year low of 32%. "This is because people have become less clear about what they expect from work, feel less cared about by their employers, and are less connected to the company's purpose."

As a recent Harvard Business Review article stated, "Quiet Quitting Is About Bad Bosses, Not Bad Employees." The research cited in the HBR article was conducted by Zenger Folkman Analysts (2022), who looked at 360-degree feedback on over 2,000 managers from 13,000 employees since 2020.

What they found was that the "data indicates that quiet quitting is usually less about an employee's willingness to work harder and more creatively, and more about a manager's ability to build a relationship with their employees where they are not counting the minutes until quitting time."

Gallup found that managers that scored highest on the measure: "balances the need for getting results with a concern for other's needs" had the highest level of people willing to "go the extra mile" in their team, at 62%, vs. those who scored lowest, with only 20% willing to go the extra mile and 14% quiet quitting, compared to just 3% quiet quitting for the top performing managers.

So, there is a strong correlation between showing concern for others, displaying empathy, and recognising work / life balance and the willingness of employees to put in discretionary effort.

Discretionary effort can have a huge impact on organisational performance: "If you have 10 direct reports and they each give 10% additional effort, the net results of that additional effort are increased productivity." (HBR.org).

A poll by Partners In Leadership confirms that when employees are happier at work, 85% say they take more initiative; 73% say they are better collaborators; and 48% care more about their work. Effective leaders who understand the correlation between higher levels of engagement, happiness, and productivity facilitate movement in the right direction, and people feel good about it.

And as John Whitmore noted engagement is critical to performance, "employee engagement has been proven to be linked to performance, and so all the behaviours that underpin engagement, such as collaborating, meaningful goal setting, delegating, and accountability... are critical to an organisation's success." (Whitmore 2017)

Invest Time in People

Many, if not all, managers and leaders would agree that "people are our most important resource" but how many leaders actually behave in a way that demonstrates they really mean this?

Simply put managers should spend more time on their people: focusing on setting and discussing progress against goals, giving, and receiving feedback, and getting to know their people through regular conversations.

In other words, as a leader, you need to create the environment for your people and team to excel and develop them, as the most important natural resource a company has.

To put this into practice as a leader you need to recognise the importance of harnessing the talent of teams in a flexible way, not a rigid hierarchical way. You need to support the building of a learning culture and then get out of the way to empower people by having a shared purpose, clear goals, a first-class support structure, protecting the team, and unlocking the resources needed for success.

Using The Empowering Leader model will create a virtuous circle to free up time for you to focus on your people and the team by creating an engaged, motivated team that is empowered and getting on with things. We can unlock potential and discretionary effort by creating a shared purpose that increases commitment and passion of employees for their work.

Passion is a much-overused word these days, it is great if you can inspire and generate passion, but it's not going to happen in the majority of jobs just because you use the words or want it to happen. Most people are not lucky enough to work on the thing they are most passionate about so if we want to engender passion at work, we need to work hard at it. There needs to be a genuine effort on the part of the business and the leadership by focusing on their people and helping to create the right environment.

As will become clear by focusing on people through the model of leadership recommended here and specifically by establishing a shared purpose and safe learning culture you will create engagement and have a much greater chance of generating passion.

Collaboration is Critical

Cooperative and collaborative work is now the norm in most organisations, meaning success is more dependent than ever on effective collaboration and teamwork. One study, found that "the time spent by managers and employees in collaborative activities has ballooned by 50 percent or more over the last two decades" (HBR.org 2016) and in many companies, more than three-quarters of an employee's day is spent communicating with colleagues.

To be successful as an organisation and as a leader we need to build high performance teams that can innovate, problem solve and find solutions quicker than the competition, and to do this they need to be able to work in a learning culture.

Work today requires a high degree of flexibility and collaboration, creating the need to employ small flexible teams regularly, based on the skills required outside of a traditional hierarchical and siloed structure. This often requires teams to form quickly and be able to adopt a learning style culture in order to be effective. So, the more experience people have of working in high performing learning teams the easier it will be for them to form the right culture and environment to succeed in each new team they join.

Harnessing the full potential of individuals is powerful, harnessing the full potential of teams is exponentially powerful. You can't unlock individual potential and create high performance teams without empowering people to take responsibility, make decisions and to act.

Key Take Aways

- You can't command and control your way to success
- Success comes from self-managed teams with the freedom and ability to get things done
- Too much structure gets in the way of responsiveness and creativity
- Create small agile and responsive teams with high levels of autonomy that cooperate across the organisation
- Build a learning organisation with a culture that supports open communication, so that things can be learned
- Employees want companies with a sense of purpose beyond the bottom line and shareholder value
- Employees want leaders who care and who balance the

drive for results with concern for other's needs, work life
balance and respect for individuals

2. High Performance Teams

"Great teams do not hold back with one another. They are unafraid to air their dirty laundry. They admit their mistakes, their weaknesses and their concerns without fear of reprisal."

Patrick Lencioni

What Do We mean by High Performing teams?

A high performing team is one that consistently delivers better results and does so within a culture and environment that makes high performance repeatable and sustainable.

Defining a high performing team is relative and to some extent subjective. The performance of a team needs to be benchmarked against something, usually past performance as well as other teams in the same industry or company.

Typically, the results a team produces against its objectives, targets or competitive set are used as the basis for judging performance. This is measuring the output of the team, based on what they do. This could be sales revenue, units produced, calls answered, or clients contacted, and it may have a time element. This is an important part of judging performance. It is a fairly objective assuming the right objectives, metrics, or benchmarks have been set on which to measure the output performance.

The other key element is how the team produces results. Looking at the way the team works and the culture in which the output is created, e.g., the levels of engagement, motivation, collaboration, and customer service. These are measured through staff surveys, customer surveys and 360-degree feedback.

This measure is important because it gives an indication of the quality of the output produced by the team. It gives a guide as to the likelihood that the superior results can be sustained over time and the degree to which results are achieved ethically, to the satisfaction of customers and within the confines of any regulations or best practice of the industry in question.

Measuring how the output results are achieved along with what has been achieved, is an important part of defining high performance.

This is because you want the performance to be sustained over time, you want the results to be ethical and stand up to scrutiny, and you want to ensure that the results are achieved on the basis of building long term customer and stakeholder relationships rather than burning bridges and creating dissatisfaction through short term expediency.

The majority of modern work is increasingly team-based, or collaborative in nature, be it in a permanent team, cross functional working group, or project team.

If a company wants to outstrip its competitors, it needs to influence not only how people work but also how they work together. So, the focus on how teams work together in order to deliver better results is critical to deliver the class leading output results, as is the leaders' role in team.

A high performing team, then, is a team that consistently delivers better results and does so within a culture and environment that makes its high performance repeatable and sustainable.

What Makes a High-Performance Team

An organisation is made up of its people. A business organisation is rarely a group of individuals, but rather a mix of, informal groupings and the most important subset, the formal team.

The teams within an organisation reflect the people in them and the leadership of the team. If you want to change organisational culture teams are the key group within the business in which to affect change.

Changing culture at an organisational level, once the organisation is large enough to be divided into distinct teams, is incredibly difficult, but through the structure of teams it becomes much more manageable.

The key to unlocking change is ensuring you have the right kind of leadership. Not because I believe in the all-knowing leader who can change things through sheer force of personality, but because I believe in the empowering leader who can help create the environment in which a high performing team can emerge and thrive.

We will cover the role of leaders in much more detail, for now we will consider what the key ingredients of a high performing team are. When considering the traits of high performing teams, you will start to realise, I hope, what kind of leadership is required and just as importantly, what needs to be avoided.

The most telling and convincing research I have seen on what makes a team outperform other teams, is the work carried out in Google, through Project Aristotle, around 20014 – 2016.

Why is it compelling? It is compelling because Google have a lot of data, so therefore the research was data driven, the research was conducted by Harvard researchers who did not have a time limit imposed, they kept going until they found an answer.

It's Not About Individuals

Another fascinating thing about the Google Aristotle research was the fact that they could not find conclusive or even a statistically relevant correlation between the "quality" of individuals in the team and the team's performance.

In other words, something other than the intelligence, knowledge or skills of individuals is driving high performance.

Clearly the quality of individuals and their performance is important, and we all want talented individuals in our team. The question that Google was asking is how you create a team whose performance is greater than the sum of its parts. What is the secret sauce that transforms a group of individuals into a high performing team. The acknowledgment of a team behind the individual is, I believe, less acknowledged in business than it is in sports. We see in sports that the team is often at the fore and individual achievers are the first to acknowledge the team. This is because no success is truly individual. Even if we take the most individual of sports, where it is one on one, such as tennis or boxing, we know that the success of the individual is due to not only their hard work but the work of many others. In the case of formula one many hundreds of people support each individual driver.

In the West, at least, we seem to find it hard to fully acknowledge the fundamental and underlying importance of the team in business settings. There is often a mention for the team, but do leaders really focus on the team first or do they focus on individual glory and the team second, if at all?

I think this fundamentally boils down to the personal insecurity of many people in leadership positions. Both psychological insecurity and position insecurity. They feel at any time they could be ousted in favour of someone else if they personally do not perform and there is a high level of imposter syndrome driving people to believe they are not really worthy, therefore they need to protect their position through ensuring their personal pre-eminence within the organisation. The irony is that if they truly focused on the team, they would improve their performance and their job would be safe.

Google's Project Aristotle

The reality is that genuinely great performance is driven and delivered by high performing teams, not individuals. Google's project Aristotle spent over two years looking for the key "ingredients" that set apart high performing teams from other teams.

The Google Aristotle researchers couldn't find any significant correlation between the performance of the team and the individuals who made up the team. "We looked at 180 teams from all over the company. We had lots of data, but there was nothing showing that a mix of specific personality types or skills or backgrounds made any difference. The 'who' part of the equation didn't seem to matter." (Duhigg, nytimes.com,2016)

With masses of data, Harvard educated psychologists and Google data analytics capabilities what they did land on was the conclusion that High Performing teams are "Learning Teams". The research noted that learning teams are, "highly motivated and go beyond their comfort zones to achieve success together. They can learn together, continually improve, innovate, and outperform other teams" (Duhigg, nytimes.com, 2016).

Prof David Clutterbuck found in recent study (2020) with a major multinational tech firm as per the findings in Google's study, that high performing teams are learning teams. He defines a learning team as: "A group of people with a shared purpose, who take responsibility for developing each other and themselves."

What interested the Google researchers was that the teams that did well on one assignment usually did well on all the others. Conversely, teams that failed at one thing seemed to fail at everything. "The researchers eventually concluded that what distinguished the "good" teams from the dysfunctional groups was how teammates treated one another. The right norms, in other words, could raise a group's collective intelligence, whereas the wrong norms could hobble a team, even if, individually, all the members were exceptionally bright." (Duhigg, nytimes.com, 2016)

They noted that these norms and ways of treating each other shared by the high performing learning teams could be summarised as the teams having, high levels of Psychological Safety. A group culture with high instances of "conversational turn-taking" (i.e., everyone has a voice). and high levels of "average social sensitivity" (empathy) within the group

Harvard Business School professor Amy Edmondson defines psychological safety as: "A shared belief held by members of a team that the team is safe for interpersonal risk taking" (Edmundson, 2018).

And in the Google study the researchers found that psychological or emotional safety was manifest in the culture of high performing teams. They found that the best performing teams had working cultures that encouraged people to get involved and share their thoughts, and which was "free from fear and ego, where people can speak up, make mistakes, question things, and raise concerns without humiliation or retribution." (Duhigg, nytimes.com, 2016)

High performance teams are learning teams, that have a positive, supportive culture with high levels of psychological or emotional safety.

Collective Intelligence

A study conducted by a group of psychologists from Carnegie Mellon, M.I.T. and Union College published in the Journal of Science (2010) supports the findings from Google's project Aristotle. The study focused on asking if there is a collective I. Q. that emerges within a team that is distinct from the intelligence of any single member.

Before this study there had not been a systematic examination of whether a "collective intelligence" exists for groups of people, beyond the individual group members. The study found: "...we find converging evidence of a general collective intelligence factor that explains a group's performance on a wide variety of tasks. This "c factor" is not strongly correlated with the average or maximum individual intelligence of group members but is correlated with the average social sensitivity of group members, the equality in distribution of conversational turn-taking…"

The conclusion we can reach is that the makeup of the individual's skills, personality and background have little or no statistical correlation to team performance, but what is strongly correlated to high performance is the way the team operates as a unit and how the team treat one another. Creating a culture of emotional safety where views, opinions, mistakes, and failures can be shared openly in a safe environment. The team can learn and grow together and capitalise on the collective intelligence of the group to deliver better performance, consistently over time.

I just want to note here, that organisations still need rules, ethical guidelines, and strong governance. Clearly if the mistake or failure is something that goes against any of these things then it needs to be dealt with in the appropriate way through the organisation's disciplinary and other relevant procedures. But in a company with high levels of psychological safety and interpersonal trust there should be less instances of this kind and certainly less catastrophic instances due to cover up and denial.

The Importance of Emotional Safety

Building a culture where people feel psychologically or emotionally safe to speak up and be honest boosts motivation, engagement, and performance. It creates a culture where learning can happen, and creativity and innovation can thrive.

Happier, motivated workers who feel a sense of connection and who feel safe to be themselves at work make for better performance. Emotional safety plays a critical role in delivering inclusivity in the workplace, by definition if you have high levels of psychological safety you are going to have higher levels of inclusivity.

In a study published in the Journal of Organizational Behaviour (2016). Professor Hood et al noted that, "Researchers are finding that psychological safety may be the No. 1 aspect of successful teams, driving creativity and innovation."

The Google research team found the level of "conversational turn taking" evident in a team was a predeterminate in high performing teams. Giving all members of the team a chance to say their piece, implies mutual respect and trust as well as an emphasis on listening and learning in the team culture. None of which is possible if the relationships in the team do not reach beyond transactional.

The Characteristics of a High-Performance Team

These teams have a number of characteristics, some of which came out as clear drivers of performance in the research on team performance and collective intelligence. There are a number of other traits that help deliver the right culture and team norms to drive high performance from a team.

As Clutterbuck's recent work on teams and team coaching found. Clutterbuck's work in a major global tech firm (2020) led him to identify these key traits which start to pull together the ingredients for a successful team. Which are:

1. Recruit the right people.
2. Utilise individual strengths for the team.
3. Use failure productively as a group.
4. Trust and respect for each other.
5. A positive attitude to change.
6. Team "buzz".
7. A leader secure in themselves.

Clutterbuck's findings echo the work of the Google Aristotle project. He notes the importance of trusting each other and psychological safety within the team, to enable "using failure productively as a group" and without these things present in the team creating a genuine team buzz and can-do positive attitude is not possible.

A Word on Recruitment

In his work Clutterbuck found that the tech company spent a lot of time, energy and resource and ensuring they recruited the right people. Getting it right at the beginning of the process, whilst time consuming and potentially frustrating, is one of the best ways of ensuring the right kind of people enter the organisation and team. It is not fool proof, but it can certainly help you achieve the culture you want to achieve.

In recruiting we often see written in job descriptions or advertisements, that cultural or organisational fit is really important. There is good reason for this as it generally means people will feel more at home in the company and they will work well with those already there. It is important to guard against cultural homogeneity and recruiting in your own image, however. This can lead to its own problems were everyone who is recruited is very similar and the level of challenge, debate and alternative viewpoints is reduced.

So, you need to build steps into your recruitment process to ensure that whilst cultural fit is tested for, there is a sufficient check on ensuring not everyone is the same. You should be looking to recruit some people who still fit with the values you espouse but who will also challenge and disrupt, to some extent, in the way they think and ask questions.

Different industry experience, different life experience, different cultures all help to enrich cultural diversity. Shared values are what you should measure to check for cultural fit, nothing else, not dress sense or tastes, or looks or any of the obviously illegal discriminatory factors.

You can check against cultural homogeneity in your recruitment process by being aware of the biases you may have or that may be prevalent in the business. Assuming the candidate ticks the boxes on values, skills, and experience, you can build questions into your standard interview process that allow the candidate to express their views on a variety of issues and questions which test for conformity and willingness to state their own opinion even if it goes against the cultural norms.

Using different people in the interview process can also make a big difference, such as asking a member of a different team to interview the candidate to bring a fresh perspective.

What is an autonomous or self-managed team?

One outcome of building a high performance learning team is that the team becomes a largely self-managed or autonomous team. A high level of autonomy for the team is an inevitable conclusion of building a high performance culture (as defined above) and of having a leader who gets out of the way and enables the team to work together to achieve their goals. Having identified the key elements that make up high performing teams, the final definition I want to cover is what I mean by a self-managed or autonomous team.

We can all imagine as a leader the twin fears of letting your team become self-managed and autonomous.

Firstly, you may ask yourself if the team is managing itself what is my role? Secondly, you may be thinking that sounds like a recipe for disaster, where's the control?

These are both very rational and important questions to ask.

Thinking about a team as self-managed is a long way from the traditional view of management and leadership, where the leader is central to the whole thing and without them the team couldn't possibly function.

This is still the view of many and the sense you get from a lot of leaders is that they need to be involved in all decision making and that the team is dependent upon them. We all know the leaders who feel they can't take a holiday or if they do take a holiday, they have to be contactable all the time because the team needs them and can't cope without them. The psychological need of the leader to feel they are in control and indispensable to the team often drives this type of leadership.

Many leaders struggle to let go of control, they have trust issues so they don't delegate decision making, they are insecure about their position and therefore feel the need to constantly prove they are needed and that the team couldn't manage without them. They may also, as a result, take personal credit for a lot of things rather than give credit to the team and individuals within it.

Think about what this kind of leadership is saying about the team. It is effectively writing the team off as a bunch of people who can't make their own decisions and who are dependent upon one person, without whom they would cease to function effectively.

Does this sound like a the right definition for a team of talented, mature adults who are experts in their chosen field and who are very capable in their roles? If it does sound like the right description then you need to change something because this is not the definition of a high functioning, high performing team.

Think about what we are saying if we believe the leader has to control the team, make all the decisions and is the indispensable cog without which the team falls apart.

What we are saying is that the team members have no real agency, that they are not capable of making decisions, that they are dependent on one person, and they are not independent experts in their role, but rather they only exist whilst the leader is place. This clearly doesn't make sense unless you are in a cult.

The self-managed team comes about through building the right culture to create learning teams with high levels of psychological safety as we have seen. A high level of autonomy for the team is an inevitable conclusion of building the right team culture and having a leader who is an integral part of the learning team culture and gets out of the way to allow individuals and the team to perform and do their jobs. The leader provides direction and support, champions the team, secures resources, and makes decisions when needed.

Key Takeaways

- High performance teams are learning teams
- Learning teams have high levels of emotional safety
- It is how the team works together and the strength of culture that drives high performance
- Great individuals alone cannot drive high performance in a team
- The team is the critical component of the organisation to drive performance and cultural change
- Leaders play a critical role in creating the right culture for high performance teams

3. The Empowering Leader

"Leaders become great not because of their power, but because of their ability to empower others."

John C Maxwell

The Role of the Leader in High Performing Teams

The leader plays a pivotal role in the realisation of high performance self-managed teams.

The world is becoming increasingly complex and uncertain and the problems facing organisations and their leadership are becoming ever more difficult to navigate. Task complexity is increasing exponentially (Schein and Schein 2018), and generational changes in what people want and expect from work have changed drastically in the last decade or so, which recent surveys highlight just what is important to millennial and Gen Z employees, particularly after the COVID pandemic:

"Employers that listen to employees with empathy and support continual learning, will be more successful in retaining employees and delivering success." (IBM Institute for Business Value 2021)

Facing into the disruptive future, leaders are going to have to have the personal capabilities to manage themselves and manage their own emotions, as well as the workplace competencies that help them do the job, such as problem-solving, collaboration, scenario thinking and making decisions.

"Employees reporting greater levels of innovation, engagement, retention, and inclusivity when working with a leader who displayed empathy." (Forbes, Catalyst 2021)

The notion that the leader is the all-knowing inspirational sage that we follow because they are somehow better is not one that is sustainable or one that will drive competitive advantage because it doesn't unlock the collective potential of the many, it doesn't create an environment where creativity and innovation can outstrip the competition. In short, these kinds of leaders do not create learning organisations, and that is what we need to succeed.

As Amy Edmundson describes in her book The Fearless Organisation (2018), many leaders are seen as authority figures who know best, however in organisations with high levels of psychological safety leaders set direction and goals and encourage people to contribute ideas and insight and lead their own work or projects autonomously with high levels of empowerment and the requisite support that people need to be truly empowered.

A learning organisation is built up of learning teams, led by people who are integral part of the team. Leaders who set direction, support, learn with, empower, and facilitate the availability of resource and influence.

Future Leaders

Future leaders will need to be both more open to new ideas and aware of their own limitations "Creating the best culture to cope with disruption requires that leaders be the students of change and invite their teams to be curious with them," (Grant Thornton, 2022) In the same report Rohit Talwar, CEO of Fast Future notes that "the ability to adapt requires a number of leadership skills which may previously have been less important."

Leaders need to be aware that they don't have all the answers and are open to learning from others to ensure make the best decisions possible. What we need to move towards is a leadership style with relationships at its core so that leaders are invested in their people. As Clutterbuck (2020) found in his research the best leaders take an interest in their people and make time for them. This will move them from the transactional to a personal cooperative mode where the leader trusts the team and the team trusts the leader.

As a leader you should be secure enough in yourself to welcome challenges and divergent opinions, only then are you going to be able to welcome in people who can help move the team on and encouraging learning through challenge.

As part of its research into what makes a great leader of high-performance teams, the Google researchers reviewed the comments on the performance ratings in employee surveys and found ten behaviours that were repeatedly attributed to the great managers. They also conducted double-blind interviews with a group of the best and worst managers to find concrete examples of what the managers were doing differently. The found the following:

- Is a good coach
- Empowers the team and does not micromanage
- Creates an inclusive team environment, showing concern for success and well-being

- Is productive and results-oriented
- Is a good communicator—one who listens and shares information
- Supports career development and discusses performance
- Has a clear vision/strategy for the team
- Has key technical skills to help advise and direct the team
- Collaborates across the organization
- Is a strong decision maker

Decisiveness is a critical leadership trait, but how you get to those decisions is markedly different in a world where the leader is part of the team, is open to hearing views, gives everyone the chance to share, and is agile in their thinking. Yes, leaders need to make the big decisions. Decision making with shared accountability is a critical leadership trait.

As Satya Nadella (Microsoft CEO) says, as a leader you need to "Listen more, talk less and be decisive when the time comes." (WallStreetJournal.com)

The Secure Leader

In order for leaders to demonstrate these behaviours they need to be secure in themselves, to not feel the need to control and to have the confidence to get out of the way.

Emotionally secure people have good emotional self-control and are emotionally stable people. They are in control of their emotions and not controlled by them. This emotional control and resilience mean that they will come across as calm, self-assured and in control. They are in tune with their emotions and recognise them for what they are, but they are one step removed from them and therefore they usually don't let their emotions get the better of them.

Managing how you react to others is critical if you want to build high levels of emotional safety and have people trust you and tell you the truth. By being able to control your emotions you can adopt reassuring and encouraging body language and facial expressions that encourage people to open up and relax. This state means people are their most honest and most creative because their mind is not blocked by fears of saying the wrong thing or getting into trouble.

Empowering Leadership

A leader who has the intention to develop skills and behaviours of their team members so that individuals and the team can increase performance. These leaders are focused on building an effective learning culture, with emotional safety and empowering the team. They are focused on the success of the team, of which they are a part, rather than their own power and position.

What Traits do they Have?

- High levels of self-awareness and the ability to manage their emotional state
- Take a personal interest in others
- Low personal ego - successful when their team is successful
- Learn through two-way feedback
- Employ empathy, actively listen, and treat people with respect
- Empower people with appropriate support
- Set clear goals and expectations

- Use coaching and mentoring to develop and guide
- A growth and learning mindset

And as the Google research found has the core leadership skills to:

- Has a clear vision/strategy for the team
- Has key technical skills to help advise and direct the team
- Collaborates across the organization
- Is a strong decision maker

Leadership needs to move from a transactional, leader-follower basis, with an emphasis on individual performance and power, to leadership based on empowering individuals to work collaboratively in a learning environment where continual improvement and innovation can thrive.

Future leaders will be required to develop a team with a shared purpose and vision and then empower them to do their job, learn and deliver. Motivating, giving direction, and inspiring the team through listening, enabling, being decisive, and providing resource, and support to the team.

It is perhaps not what you believe or have been taught that leadership is. You might ask how can I be the leader and be part of the team?

This is not an easy line to walk, but it is possible if you are emotionally secure and have the self-belief to work as a member of the team whilst still being able to give direction, make tough decisions and discipline when necessary. It's not about being friends with everyone, it is about getting to know them, respecting them, caring about them as individuals and valuing each person's contribution and opinions.

It's about building trust and mutual respect, allowing everyone a voice, playing to people's strengths and an open communication style. You still need employ the skills of time management, meeting etiquette, decision making and planning to ensure the team has forward momentum. I am not advocating a free for all or teams without structure.

Key Takeaways

- Leaders play a pivotal role in the realisation of high-performance teams
- Leaders need personal capabilities manage their own emotions
- They set direction, guide, support, protect, share responsibility, learn, and facilitate access to resource and influence the teams need to succeed
- They build trust by getting to know their team, respecting them, and caring about them and valuing each person's contribution and opinions
- They need keys skills: listening, problem-solving, collaboration, big picture thinking, scenario thinking, and making decisions are key
- The leader doesn't need to know it all, can admit when they don't know and ask for help
- Leaders should build relationships, provide support, resources, direction, and decisiveness and then Get Out of the Way
- Leaders are successful when the team is successful, and the gain influence and power through their team's performance

4. Principle 1 – It Starts with You

> "Self-awareness gives you the capacity to learn from your mistakes as well as your successes. It enables you to keep growing."
>
> *Lawrence Bossidy*

It's All About Behaviours

One of the best pieces of insight I had as a young ambitious junior manager was that as I progressed through the layers of leadership it became more and more about behaviours and less about task or functional skills. Functional knowledge and skills are the bedrock of a successful career, but leadership is about the way you think and the way you behave. Behaviour and thought are inextricably linked, which is the basis of cognitive behavioural theory of therapy, the way we behave effects the way we think and the way we think has a marked effect on behaviour.

Leaders should be paid for their thinking and behaviours. Yes, they need a foundation of fundamental skills, knowledge, and experience behind them, but we should recruit, and reward leaders based on their mind and their behavioural skills.

The quality of their thinking impacts on vision, strategic planning and decision making and their behaviour impacts on how they communicate, inspire, and motivate. Your effectiveness on these two metrics is how your leadership ability will be judged.

As a leader I was often asked by very good technical employees who were highly skilled, and highly knowledgeable why they were not promoted into leadership roles, but others were who were not as good at sales, marketing, or operations technically did get the promotions. These people were often frustrated at their lack of progress into management or senior leadership roles.

In discussing this sensitive topic, I used what I've come to call a career bar. It's something I initially sketched on a piece of paper when talking to a member of my team who was frustrated and wanted a promotion into a leadership role. I used it to highlight the difference in emphasis between technical skills and behaviours as you progress into leadership roles.

It became a useful tool that allowed me to explain the fundamental difference of what we were looking for in managers and what people needed to demonstrate in order to progress from exceptional technical performers. I found that most people were able to understand it quite easily and it helped make it clear to them in unemotive terms why they were not yet in a leadership role. It is a jumping off point to talk about where they need to focus their development.

Technical, Functional, Individual Contributor

Technical Skills & Knowledge   Behaviour

Leadership Role

Technical Skills & Knowledge   Behaviour

What this simple bar illustrates is the extent to which it becomes about behaviours and the way you think once you are in a leadership role. To be a successful leader you first need to grasp this and understand the fundamental importance of it to your role.

Secondly you have to know what kind of thinking and behaviours are critical to your role as a leader. Finally, you need to be self-aware enough to understand your own performance against the desired behaviours and importantly, which behaviours and thinking models you need to stop, modify, or start.

It is often the case that as you progress in your leadership journey, as well as learning new ways of thinking and behaviours, you are going to have to unlearn some, if not many, of the things that got you to where you are. In many cases they are behaviours we have managed to get away with but that will hold you back from being truly successful as a leader.

Stop, Modify and Start

Many of us believe in our own myth and we are blind to the effect our behaviours have on others, especially if we are successful. If we are a success, we naturally tend not to question our behaviours or look too deeply at ourselves, "it's working" we think to ourselves.

Even in the face of feedback we can convince ourselves that the feedback is just an opinion and is not relevant. But to be successful as leader today, to build employee engagement and to gain discretionary effort from your team, you need to be aware of how your behaviours impact others and how they may negatively affect your ability to inspire and engage.

Whilst working as a coach with a leader who is very successful and an inspiration to many it was clear that this leader was highly rational, very organised, and extremely focused on controlling the agenda.

These were behavioural traits that had been successful in many ways over the years but became a block to success when dealing with a global management team and Country leaders from different cultures. This CEO wanted to better engage and motivate these leaders, who were critical to the business's success but who were not fully aligned to the central vision and who were expressing frustration regarding communication with central head office.

Through coaching, the leader became aware of the behaviours that were preventing him from building strong relationships and communicating effectively with these crucial stakeholders. The effect of his behaviour was to make the local MDs feel as though their voices were not heard and that they were not listened to. The highly planned tightly controlled meetings meant there was never enough time for debate, they also felt there was no time to raise issues, concerns, or challenges.

The behaviours of the CEO that were ideal when the company was in initial start-up mode and that were still useful for corporate governance meetings and investor briefings were not optimal when running an international organisation with local affiliate organisations from differing cultures. More time was built into the meetings to listen and debate, open sessions were introduced to allow the airing of issues and challenges, in addition more one to one contact points with the local MDs were set up. This behavioural shift and the changes made because of it, greatly improved the quality of relationships and the effectiveness of the global team.

I'm sure we have all worked for the type A, extrovert boss (you may be one yourself) who is decisive, driven, and full of can-do spirit. These are great leadership traits but, in my experience, the same type of boss is not necessarily good at listening, may be slow to change course when their strategy is not working (despite evidence to the contrary) and can come across as disrespectful of others time and opinions. This can create resentment, it may stop people speaking up for fear of being shot down or ignored and it definitely leads to poorer decision making, there is no one leader on the planet who has the best ideas all of the time.

We are aiming to create a learning organisation, made up of high performing learning teams, we need leaders who learn and empower to make that happen. Who are aware of their own behaviours, who take feedback and who are willing to stop, modify or start new behaviours to get the best out their people for the ultimate benefit of the organisation.

Self-Awareness

Being emotionally secure and in control your emotions are important traits for a leader who is successful in engaging and motivating their team. In order become more secure and emotionally stable you need to know yourself; you need to be self-aware. As a leader you have to be able to be honest with yourself, about your strengths and weaknesses and you need to be cognisant of those behaviours and ways of thinking that are not optimal for successful Empowering leadership. As Daniel Goleman states "… if you don't have self-awareness… if you can't have empathy and have effective relationships, then no matter how smart you are, you are not going to get very far." [2018]

In order to be more self-aware, you first have to want to understand yourself and be comfortable with being honest about the areas where your behaviour is not what it should be. In understanding ourselves more fully we need to become aware of the blind spots and biases we all have. All of us have blind spots and biases. Areas of our behaviour or ways of thinking that we may not be consciously aware of, but that cause to think and behave in a certain way in specific circumstances. Becoming consciously aware of these is critical in becoming more self-aware.

When we are consciously aware of our biases and prejudices, we can at least begin to think about how we change the way we think and behave to improve the outcomes.

So how to become more self-aware? There are a number of things we can do to become more self-aware, first of all you need to practice self-reflection, open up to others and seek feedback, practice active listening, and develop a Growth Mindset. We will cover these things as we go through the book.

Growth Mindset
What is Growth Mindset?

A growth mindset is the belief that a person's capacities and talents can be improved over time and are not fixed. The theory was developed by Stanford psychologist Carol Dweck and explained in her 2006 book "Mindset: The New Psychology of Success".

Underpinning the idea is the belief that skills and intelligence can be improved with effort and persistence and that we are not fixed with a certain level of intelligence or innate ability at birth.

Dweck found that some people have a fixed mindset, whilst others exhibit a growth mindset, and people can therefore be placed on a spectrum from having a fixed to a growth mindset.

She found there were two main approaches that people take:

1.   I won't be good at that, so I won't bother trying, because I don't want to fail or look silly trying and expose myself to others criticism

2.   I may not be good at it the first time, but let's give it a go and I will learn and get better through effort, persistence, and reflection

People with a growth mindset embrace challenges, build resilience through perseverance when faced with hurdles, learn from constructive criticism and mistakes, and take inspiration from others.

As Dweck summed up, "In a growth mindset, challenges are exciting rather than threatening. So, rather than thinking, I'm going to reveal my weaknesses, you say, here's a chance to grow." (2006)

Those with a growth mindset believe "intelligence can be developed" and their abilities can be enhanced through the learning process (Bates, Bob 2016). They understand that their talents and abilities can be developed through effort, teaching, coaching and persistence. It is not about thinking everyone can become the very best at everything or that everyone can be as good as everyone else, but it's about believing everyone has the ability to learn if the put in the time and effort.

Those with a fixed mindset tend to see things as in a deterministic way and have a belief in natural ability and innate talents, that you either have or you don't, but for someone with a fixed mindset you can grow or improve if you don't have the talent, so hard work and perseverance will not be rewarded with growth and success. Their sense of self is tied up in how well they perform and how few mistakes they make, they feel like one mistake or failure could brand them as useless for the rest of their life's. This leads them to seek approval from others to reinforce their self-image and protect their egos.

Why it is Important for Leaders

It is important to adopt this kind of mindset and approach to the world as much as possible to be a successful, creative, and empowering leader. A growth mindset is associated with consistently learning from success and mistakes to improve performance. The mindset is one of continual improvement and of believing no matter how good you are, you can always do better. This is the drive that leads to a learning culture where innovation can thrive.

Adopting a growth mindset

Individuals may not necessarily be aware of their own mindset, but their mindset can still be discerned based on their behaviour. It is especially evident in their reaction to failure. Fixed-mindset individuals dread failure because it is a negative statement on their basic abilities, while growth mindset individuals don't mind or fear failure as much because they realize their performance can be improved, they are either winning or learning!

Adopting or improving your growth mindset is possible, having a fixed mindset is not "fixed". But changing to a growth mindset from a fixed one takes work. We can train our brain to think more in a growth mindset kind of way. To do so you need be aware of your own thought patterns and habits, and you need to be willing to step outside your comfort zone to accommodate changes.

Developing your way of thinking and your mindset as a leader:

You don't need to know it all

Internalising the fact that you do not need to be perfect as a leader and you do not need to know everything is critical, not only for success, but for your mental health.

Being perfect or having all the answers should not even be a goal, it's not possible nor is it desirable.

Perfectionists tend to be micro managers who are afraid to delegate and empower, they also tend to procrastinate for fear of getting their decision wrong or it not being perfect. No one knows everything, which is why great leaders surround themselves with great people, they admit what they don't know, and they listen to understand and learn.

Don't seek others approval

This is a difficult one for many people, if not most people, to a greater or lesser extent. We often obsess over what people think of us, in work it is usually our boss or the "higher ups", but also, as a leader, it is our team.

Let me stress it is important to be aware of how you come across as a leader and you should be conscious of the words you choose and the behaviours you display. However, your motivation should not be to seek others approval, it should be because it is what you believe is the best way to be successful as a leader.

Seeking others' approval can prevent us from learning, and from getting to the best solutions. It can stifle innovation and stop you trying things because you fear what other will think.

Purpose and Long-Term Goals

Having a sense of purpose leads to setting goals for the longer term. This helps provide direction and motivation by giving us a reason to keep going, to keep trying and to keep learning. If we set learning objectives, we will be open to new experiences that help us grow. It takes time to grow and achieve meaningful goals. Learning a new behaviour and changing the way we think is like learning to play a new instrument, it's a journey and it takes practice. A growth mindset teaches you that progress and effort towards success are what's important, not how long it takes.

Learning Opportunities

Look at failure, rejection, and mistakes as learning opportunities. That's not to say we don't lick our wounds and we definitely need to reflect. So, take the time you need to get over the initial disappointment but then you need to learn and move on.

There will be times when you make mistakes or don't perform well. People will give you feedback and tell you how to do better. Don't look at feedback as a criticism of your abilities. Be open to suggestions, take on what you can and move on.

Professional sports people are brilliant at this, they need to be able to go through this whole process very quickly during the course of a game! The very best can move on from an error or disappointment immediately or in seconds, putting it behind them to focus on the game. Even the great Roger Federer had unforced errors in every single game of tennis he ever played, but he was able to leave them behind move on and focus on the next shot. After the game the reflection and learning process takes place, but not a process of recrimination or dwelling on the error or disappointment, merely asking "what can I learn from this? And how do I put it into practice?".

Open Up, Listen and Seek Feedback

A secure leader seeks feedback, they actively listen to the opinion of others, and they reflect on what they hear.

Someone said to me whilst discussing leadership that "it is difficult for leaders to get good feedback because the people who work for them won't feel comfortable giving feedback."

This is exactly why we need to move to a new kind of leadership, as a leader you need to create a culture and environment where people do feel they can give you honest feedback and speak their mind. Within the correct boundaries and with respect, but honest and open all the same.

As a leader only you can set the environment where this becomes possible. By your behaviour, actions, and words you will demonstrate that you do accept feedback, and that you do listen and that the person giving constructive feedback in an appropriate way will not face any negative consequences.

Opening yourself up to feedback, and admitting what you don't know is showing vulnerability, it is letting others know that you know that you're not perfect, that you don't have all the answers and that you need, and will accept, help. Vulnerability in leaders is seen as a desirable trait because it makes them more human and reduces the divide between the leader and their followers, team members or employees. It is also important because as a leader it is one way of demonstrating that you are open and that in turn that encourages open dialogue and honesty from people.

It is a positive trait of leaders to actively demonstrate a growth mindset and to show some vulnerability in terms of not having all the answers and needing help and support. But always remember we are talking about vulnerability in a work context, as a leader, we should not confuse this definition of vulnerability in leaders with being emotionally vulnerable. That is not to say leaders are never emotionally vulnerable nor that there is anything wrong with it, but if a leader is in an emotionally vulnerable state for whatever reason, then they need to seek help or take time out to deal with whatever is causing it.

How you react to that honest feedback is critical in building a culture of open dialogue and creative discussion. It takes a little bit of time for the team members to slowly work their way to being more and more open and honest but if your reaction and responses are positive and supportive, they will open up and become more emboldened so that you will get the honest feedback.

One of the obvious advantages of this is that you will get bad news early, which makes it good news, because you can do something about it. You will also be able to react to the teams needs and concerns in real time and avoid any festering problems or unintended consequences of your behaviour that you are unconscious of.

I worked with an organisation to help turn around an underperforming and demotivated sales team. This team was measured annually, not just by its internal performance but by a highly publicised and highly regarded customer survey, which rated all of the sales team in the industry on a number of performance scales. It was a measure of how well the team had built relationships, how creative they were and how responsive they were. There was a lot of cache attached to the position achieved in the survey.

The team had come 4th in the survey for the past three years despite being one of the two biggest players in the sector. After working with the team, they were placed first in the next survey, and they held that position for three years running.

To achieve the turnaround, we needed to instil a customer focused approach, establish new procedures, reorganise the team, and provide relevant training and coaching. But a big part was the change in culture brought about by the change in leadership style that was implemented.

Every member of the team was spoken to individually and encouraged to give honest feedback on their ideas on how to improve the team culture and performance. The leader actively listened, asked open questions, and did not pontificate. There was a conscious effort to listen neutrally and avoid a defensive reaction or giving counter arguments to suggestions. This demonstrated that this was a safe space for the team to be honest and to give feedback that was insightful and useful.

Specifically on the point of opening up to feedback, the senior leadership team of five were asked to think about what they would do if they were in running the team and to present their ideas to the team leader. The team were initially tentative in expressing their thoughts and ideas, but the leader encouraged them to open up and be more honest. By the end of the session, they had come up with an excellent set of strategic and tactical objectives to transform the culture and the way the team went out to customers. This became the basis of a year one strategic plan that they executed effectively to get them to first place in the customer survey.

Reflective Practice

There may be a few groans at this, with thoughts of "navel gazing" or long periods staring blankly into space. Busy, driven successful people often find they don't have time for reflection. Additionally, whilst what they are doing is successful, they may not feel the need to reflect and view it as a waste of time. However, it is not a passive exercise, and it doesn't need to take a long time, it should be focused on change and moving forward in a spirit of continual improvement.

Reflective learning comes from being able analyse, evaluate, and interpret experiences actions and feedback, in such a way as to be able to form clear actionable insights.

It's important for effective leaders to practice reflective thinking to reflect on their behaviour based on feedback, insights gained through interaction, reading or their experience.

Reflecting on your thinking, biases and behaviour helps you to better understand your own competencies, strengths, and weaknesses. It is essential to become a successful empowering leader who can build engagement and generate high performance from their team. It takes reflection to really understand how you think and behave and also to understand the impact of your behaviour and words on others, which is particularly important as a leader.

Reflection is essentially the process of learning from our own experience, actions, and thoughts, by critically reflecting on them, "to enable insights and aid learning for new personal understanding, knowledge, and action, to enhance our self-development and our professional performance." (Lawrence-Wilkes and Ashmore, 2014).

In other words, being aware of one's own thinking, biases, and knowledge to better understand our own strengths and shortcomings and to be more consciously aware of what we know and importantly of what we don't know i.e., conscious incompetence. Conscious incompetence is an important step in developing our behaviours because we become aware of what we are not good at and therefore we can set about improving it.

Without becoming consciously aware of our behaviour it's not possible to change it. We might resist feedback because of a lack of acceptance of the relevance of the feedback given and value of the change in behaviour. The other reason we may shun feedback is because we are insecure about changing a well-established behaviour that we believe has served us well and that is part of who we are.

When reflecting it helps to put a bit of structure around it, even if the whole thing only takes minutes, sometimes it may take longer. The steps below represent the thought process I go through to reflect on my behaviour proactively or based on feedback I have had. It is a simple process map to ensure your reflection is focused on discovering learnings, acting, and moving on. You don't want reflection to be a repetitive process and you don't want to get stuck reflecting on something without moving forward through the process to ensure you learn and take action. This is why I have purposefully not represented the process as a cycle, because for me each reflection needs to move you on not become a closed loop.

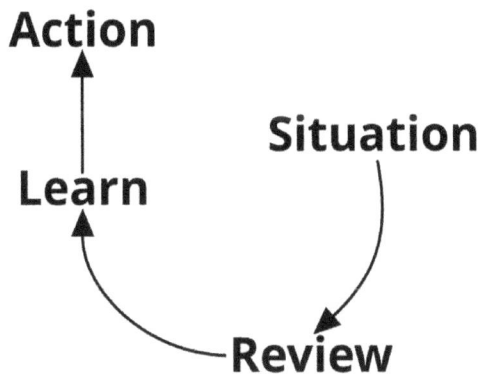

Action

Situation

Learn

Review

1. Situation

Think about the circumstances and what happened

2. Review

What was good and bad? How did I feel? How did others feel?

3. Learn

What would you differently? What would you not do next time? What else could you do?

In other words what behaviour would you Stop, Start, or Modify.

4. Act

What actions will you take? How will you progress?

What help do you need? Who can help?

One of your actions may be to share your reflective learnings with someone to seek their input and feedback.

When you come back to a similar situation your reflective practice should enable you to behave differently and hopefully more effectively, based on the learning you took from the process and the actions identified.

So, take time to reflect, seek feedback, open up to the fact that you are not perfect, and you may need to make some changes. Becoming consciously aware of the need for change is a powerful tool in your development as a leader and can help you reach greater success through improved performance of yourself and your team.

Your Objectives and Actions from this Chapter

- Start with Yourself – Think about your level of self-awareness
- Reflect on what you hear, observe and your own behaviours, body language and speech
- Think about what behaviours you need to Stop, Modify or Start
- Work on developing a Growth and Learning Mindset
- Seek Feedback and accept it openly to help you become more self-aware

5. Principle 2 – Shared Purpose

"What will become compellingly important is absolute clarity of shared purpose…"

(Dee Hock)

This book is primarily focused on becoming an empowering leader of a high-performance team, everything here applies to leaders of organisations also, but the focus of this chapter is on how you define a shared purpose with your team and set strategic objectives for your team. At an organisational level the companies Vision should be the guiding light for all strategic objectives so we will cover this in brief and describe how Purpose differs and fits in with Vision.

Vision

Most people know about Vision statements. There is a lot of confusion between vision and mission or Purpose as I have described it.

Purpose is akin to mission, in other words is what the team is there to do and why the team exists as a team. Importantly it is about what the team does that no other team does, that makes it unique in its purpose and therefore value adding to the whole.

Vision is where you are headed as a team and the road you want to take to get there. You can't very well craft a vision if you are not clear on the purpose of the team or organisation. You need to know what the team is doing and why they are doing it before you can set the vision for the future.

Visions point the way. They describe where the company wants to get to and act as a forward-looking guide to the team or organisation when setting plans and strategies. In other words, your strategic objectives should be aligned with your vision, they all should help you make progress toward your vision. If your strategic objectives do not align with your vision, then they need to be reassessed.

A memorable and engaging vision statement engages your people emotionally, and helps inspire them to go the extra mile, as well as making them feel part of something bigger than their job, which we know is an important part of engagement.

A vision statement describes the inspirational, desired future state of a business in the next 5 to 10 years and guides the direction of the organisation's effort to create what does not yet exist. It is a statement of the future big picture objective of the business.

All teams within the organisation should align with the company vision and determine and articulate their own team vision at a functional level, for example HR, Sales, Operations or Marketing. These visions must align with the organisations vision.

It is a common part of the definition of a leader that they have vision and can clearly communicate their vision. This is important, no doubt, and all leaders should be able to do "the vision thing" to some extent. But just as with all leadership traits and characteristics they are never found in every leader. If you want to develop a vision for your team, you do not have to come up with it all by yourself. As a leader and you don't have to have blinding flashes of inspiration to create a meaningful vision for the team to work towards. You can use the team to help you develop and hone your vision and this process will generate buy in, commitment and motivation from the team or organisation.

Team Purpose

If we think back to chapter one and the characteristics of high-performance learning teams, we will remember that having a shared sense of purpose was critical in knitting the team into a whole and making it feel like a true team that are all in it together.

Forming a team that knows why it exists and why it is unique is crucial to building a high performing, motivated and collaborative team. I have experienced leading a team with no real sense of purpose and can attest that developing a shared sense of purpose made a huge difference to their performance.

Working with the commercial team in a large company, I was getting to know the team and I asked them to explain what the team did, the structure, their roles, and how they fit into the structure.

The sort of answers they came up with were something like this; "I look after the internal customers, but I also have to make sure my external customers are serviced, and I work across all divisions, but I am a divisional champion for division X."

Another team member explained their role, "I don't see external customers, I work for the divisions and brief the sales team on divisional priorities and new launches, so I work for the division really, but I am part of the sales team."

These responses were representative of the team

describing a number of disparate roles in a sales team, few of which seemed to be focused on the customer. This led me to pose a question to the group.

"Who is your customer and what is your main purpose?"

One or two stated that "retailers are our customers". Some said that they seemed to be serving the internal divisions, so they were their customers.

After some debate and back and forth they came to a general conclusion that they were largely internally focused, that they didn't have a clear purpose... other than perhaps to serve the divisions and attend a lot of internal meetings justifying their existence and making divisional heads feel reassured that lots of busy work was happening on their behalf.

So, they had no clear purpose, no clear customer focus, and a high percentage of their time was spent on internal issues with a large amount of internal wheel spin preventing forward momentum and action.

You probably won't be surprised to hear that this team was underperforming its peers and was deemed to be underperforming internally, despite, or perhaps because of all of the time spent on internal matters.

The team was also unrepresented at board level, had no champion, lacked resources and importantly it had no clear direction, priorities, or purpose. Needless to say, moral was low, and wins were few and far between.

In this example one of the first things, we got the team to start talking about was their purpose as a team, with an emphasis on who their customer was.

We interviewed all of the team members, some internal stakeholders, and a large cross section of customers to find out what they wanted and how the team could gain competitive advantage. The team then used these inputs to work on defining and agreeing their purpose. Then based on their shared purpose they could start to think about strategic priorities that aligned with the purpose.

They created with a statement that encapsulated the team's role in the organisation to maximise distribution and points of interaction with potential customers. It emphasised how they would achieve their aim by providing the best solutions for customers and encapsulated what the team does that is not fulfilled by any other part of the organisation.

"To place our products in front of as many potential consumers as possible at point of sale; by creating the best customer solutions for our retail partners."

Purpose provides direction and cohesion, it helps people understand the WHY behind turning up to work, which is critical for motivation and engagement.

Think about the emotional connection and motivation driven by the statement describing a job "I make car components", compared with describing the purpose of the job "I make components that help people, and their families get safely and conveniently from A to B".

Or "I make sandwiches" compared to "I help people to enjoy nutritional, affordable and tasty lunches"

Shared Purpose

The key to defining your Purpose is to define it as a group. This means it will work as a motivational touch stone for the team because it is shared.

To be a genuinely shared purpose everyone in the team has to believe in it, they have to have bought into it, only then can they be committed to it and be motivated by it.

The best way to ensure this happens is to develop and create this with the team. It's important as a leader to have a sense of what the team's purpose is, but it is another thing to impose it without a chance for the team to input, debate and craft it together. You can do this in a fun open way that works for you and the team.

- This shared process drives a deep understanding of the why behind the team's existence not just the what.
- When people understand the why they are more motivated, when they have a shared purpose, they are more committed and engaged.
- When they are part of a team with a purpose, they are more likely to collaborate and be team players.

The fundamental questions you are asking, and answering are:

Why are we here?

Why does the company need this team?

Why do we do what we do?

Why is different to what any other team does?

As a leader your role is to input into the development of the shared purpose, to propose a start point for discussion based on your view, but it is not your role to try to push it through or manipulate the group to come to your view. Your role is to create the right environment in which people can input and debate and to put in place the right process and sufficient time to enable your team to develop a shared purpose they buy into and believe in.

Make the Time

It is worth spending time on this activity. Finding time for this kind of foundational building block of successful teams is often difficult for leaders because many leaders are too focused on the day-to-day issues, they are too concerned about perception of their boss or peers to take time out to address these things or they simply don't see the value in it because they believe in command and control.

I always found it ironic and disheartening in equal measure when working as a leader that the least successful leaders, with the most people problems, highest staff turnover and constant "crises", were the ones who couldn't find time for this kind of thing. They believed everything else was more important than building a positive, creative team culture that allowed the team to excel. These were the same leaders who constantly bemoaned having to deal with people and resented the time it took to develop and coach people or build a positive team culture. Their belief was that people should simply be getting on with their job and doing what they were supposed to do or told to do. These leaders were too busy to spend much time on their people, even though success is only possible through their people.

Don't believe the hype! There is always time to do these things. The best leaders find the time. The best leaders make the time. Empowering leaders don't get tied up in "busy work", they don't have meetings for meetings sake, they don't need to be constantly updated and briefed on everything that's happening because they have delegated, empowered, and enabled their people to get on with things.

So, make the time to get your team together to define and agree on a shared purpose.

Make it Productive and Fun

There are 4 simple steps that will get you a shared purpose you can all believe in:

1. Get the team to complete a short questionnaire to collect their initial thoughts on what they believe the purpose of the team is or should be. This can be anonymous if you think it will help elicit more honest answers.
    a. Use this data to put together a word cloud and short presentation on the initial words and phrases that are most commonly being used to describe the teams or organisation's purpose.
2. Hold a workshop with the whole team to come up with a shared purpose. Make it a fun experience and use it for team building by following up or starting with a team activity.
    a. Present the findings from the survey to the group and show what the most common words and phrases are

so far

b. Have some open debate in the large group about the findings – encourage people to get involved

c. Next split people into small groups (if needed) and get them working together to propose a shared purpose back to the group. Give them materials to use to make their presentation as interesting as possible. They should also explain why they believe this is the team's purpose and what differentiates it from other teams or organisations.

d. Each group then presents their idea back to the larger group and takes questions and comments – as the leader your job is to facilitate and ensure the tone and participation levels are appropriate

e. At the end of the session, you will have a number of different takes on the Team's Purpose. You may find the feedback clusters together naturally and it is relatively easy to find the Team Purpose.

f. If you find from the group submissions that it is not obvious what the final Purpose is – you can go through a process of voting with the group to find the most popular elements that make up the purpose. This should give you proposed Shared Purpose that you can then take away and craft into your statement of purpose to bring back to communicate back to the group.

3. Send out the final Shared Purpose to the team prior to holding a final session to discuss your Shared Purpose and

what it means for the strategic direction of the team.

4.   In this session present the final Shared Purpose and gain agreement through discussion with the team.

Discuss how it aligns with the organisations and your customers (internal and / or external) mission or purpose.

Agree how you are going to communicate it and share it. And who with? Internally only or externally as well?

Then use the session to tee up the next session on Strategic Priorities.

Your Purpose gives people a sense of belonging and a positive feeling of something bigger than their individual role. Purpose also helps guide your strategic priorities and objectives. It can be used to make sure that what you are focusing on fits with your purpose and the direction you want to head in.

Your Objectives and Actions from this Chapter

- Develop and communicate a Vision for your organisation or team
- Work with your team or organisation to define your Shared Purpose
- Make the process inclusive, iterative, fun and engaging
- Communicate you Purpose internally and externally
- Use you Purpose to help develop Strategic Objectives and Priorities

6. Principle 3 - Direction and Decision Making

"Simplicity and common sense should characterise planning and strategic direction"

(Ingvar Kamprad)

There are three "D's" in the Drive component of the model of Empowering Leadership. I'm going to cover Direction and Decisiveness in this chapter, and Delegation will be covered in the next chapter.

Direction, Decisiveness and Delegation are fundamental behaviours and skills that effective leaders need to have. These give you the ability to drive forward momentum to deliver results and if combined with the other elements of the model, will allow you to get the maximum potential out of your people.

Strategic Direction

Giving clear direction so that everybody knows what their priorities are and where they are headed is a core leadership requirement. Strategic direction is given through strategic priorities and detailed direction through effective delegation (see Chapter 7), which enables you to get out of the way and empower people to deliver against clearly understood objectives.

Once you have established a shared purpose (Chapter 5) and the team is united behind that purpose you can set your strategic priorities.

Strategic priorities give direction and guidance to everyone about what their focus should be and where to put their energy.

Your strategic priorities should create clear long-term objectives you hope to achieve over a designated period of time.

Performance and Learning Objectives

In defining high performance in Chapter 2 I noted the importance of focusing on both performance objectives and learning objectives.

In other words, measuring how people work as well as what output or results they produce, e.g., the levels of engagement, motivation, collaboration, and customer service. These are measured through staff surveys, customer surveys and 360-degree feedback.

This measure is important because it gives an indication of the quality of the output produced by the team. It gives a guide as to the likelihood that superior results can be sustained over time and the degree to which results are achieved ethically, to the satisfaction of customers and within the confines of any relevant regulations.

So, when setting strategic priorities, you need to think about not just setting performance objectives that measure output, but also learning and cultural objectives that measure how the performance is achieved.

Setting Strategic Priorities

I am not going to cover the whole of the strategic planning process in this book, there are lots of great sources for detailed strategic planning and the process of completing plan templates etc, such as: "Strategic Planning: A Practical Guide to Strategy Formulation and Execution" (B.K. Simerson)

What I want to focus on is helping you make sure your team has a clear set of priorities that gives clear direction.

The key for me, is that your strategic priorities are seen as shared priorities by the team, as with Purpose. You need their buy-in to effectively deliver your plans.

As the famous quote from Peter Drucker goes "Culture eats strategy for breakfast". In other words, the culture, your leadership behaviours, and the people implementing the plan, determine success of your strategy, regardless of how great your strategy may be on paper.

Without effective execution strategy is just a series of words.

Effective execution is delivered by people being motivated and engaged in the strategic aims so that they give of their best and work to make progress towards achieving the strategic objectives. Ensuring that people buy into the priorities and are invested in them as shared goals is a sure way to breed greater motivation and engagement.

You want your team thinking:

"Yeah, I can get behind these objectives, they fit with our purpose, they have a good chance of being successful and they fit with my ethics and principles. I'm happy and proud to share them with other people."

Any disconnect on any of these factors, as you know yourself, leads to some degree of disengagement, reduces motivation, and is unlikely to release maximum discretionary effort.

Not only should your team want to talk about your strategic priorities, but they should also be able to talk about them easily and succinctly.

Your strategic objectives should enable you, and anyone else in your team, to talk readily and easily about what they are. So, you shouldn't have too many and they shouldn't be complicated.

For example, they could include:

- Open up a new channel of distribution
- Increase web traffic by 20% over last year
- Launch a customer engagement programme
- Improve collaboration and teamwork across all areas
- Develop customer relationship skills across the team

The key areas for strategic objectives will be:
- Output performance measures e.g. sales, units shipped,

turnaround time, profit employee turnover, monthly active users, etc
- Customer measures e.g. customer satisfaction, delivery efficiency, response time etc.
- Learning and development and cultural measures e.g. Increase collaboration, engagement, or listening. Skills development and training etc.

Depending on where your team sits in the organisation you need to ensure your strategic priorities align with the organisations as a whole, with any interdependent functions in the business and where relevant with customers and/or external bodies.

Action, Accountability and Ammunition

It sounds obvious, but to succeed you and your team have to execute your strategic priorities. Remember this is where most strategies fail, it's not usually the strategy which is bad but rather it is executed badly.

One famous example of a failure to execute the strategic aims, is the merger of AOL and Time Warner, one of the biggest corporate mergers of all time.

In 1999 AOL wanted to combine their internet service business with Time Warner's entertainment and media business. AOL accessing Time Warner's massive content library and Time Warner accessing the huge AOL subscriber base.

This merger was set to make AOL Time Warner the largest entertainment company in the 21st century. Both AOL and

Time Warner had millions of subscribers. And combining those subscribers was expected to enhance to revenues estimated at $400 million. Additionally, both businesses had duplicate and redundant operations that they planned to remove through synergies, bringing estimated cost savings of $600 million.

Given these potential strategic wins merging the two businesses seemed like a sound move, so the merger was completed in the year 2000. However, despite the strategic plans making a lot of sense there were numerous flaws in the execution. The promised synergy between the two companies never appeared, ultimately leading this deal to complete failure.

The reasons behind the failure were partly to do with a shift in the market in which the companies operated with the swift growth of high-speed internet not being predicted by AOL.

But the biggest reason was their failure to execute the deal effectively so they could not realise the revenue growth of $400m and $600m cost saving synergies they had predicted. Post the deal they did not actually merge the two businesses. Instead of working together as one company to capitalise on the strategic benefits identified by merging, they continued to operate as separate businesses and were in fact in conflict with one another. Believe it or not AOL refused to carry Time Warner content, one of the key strategic aims of the merger and Time Warner had to pay market rates to AOL to reach their subscriber base thereby reducing their profit by a third.

By not combining their businesses they were also not able to realise the identified cost savings.

It is remembered as one of the worst mergers of all time. AOL Time Warner paid the price for the failure posting a massive loss one year after the merger, with the stock price for both companies crashing by 90% in the following 2 years. This is an example that shows strategy without execution is a fallacy.

This example is extreme but very real, but we can see the failure to execute manifest itself time after time in organisations of all kinds, from big strategic decisions to the more prosaic failure to implement a strategic plan properly.

For instance, in my work with organisations I came across a common example of a failure to execute a new process. This organisation set a strategic goal to save over £1m annually by reducing the number of temporary workers employed. In order to do this, they created a new authorisation process whereby they would be able to better control the use of temporary staff. It all looked good on paper and made a lot of sense. However, it was a complete failure because they did not execute it properly.

To implement a change of this nature successfully in a large complex organisation takes a huge amount of communication, explanation, and training. So much so that you should spend 2 or 3 times the amount of time drawing up your execution and communication plan as you do on *writing the strategy and process. In this case they failed to effectively communicate or train people on the new process. They had no plan. Their communication consisted of one email with a link embedded, that the vast majority of people did not even open. Needless to say, the new process did not get implemented and the savings did not materialise, but staff were however more confused and demotivated when trying to hire new staff after a change to procedure they did not understand or even know about.*

To action strategic priorities effectively someone will need to be accountable for making them happen. You should make sure that each objective has clear ownership, accountability and measurements attached to them to ensure they are executed effectively.

This is where the effective leader ensures that each of the strategic priorities has a single person who owns it, who is accountable for it and who is motivated to achieve it.

The way to do this is to involve the team in reviewing and creating strategic priorities and then through this process you can assign leads for each objective. The execution lead can then establish a delivery team as needed, which may be a cross functional team if required.

Your job as a leader is to ensure the execution lead who is accountable for actioning the objective knows what they need to do, and that they have the ammunition they need to do it in terms of sufficient resources and support.

We will cover more in terms of culture, coaching, resourcing, and championing the team in Chapters 8, 9 and 10

Giving ownership and accountability means letting go of the responsibility for devising the detailed operational plan to deliver the strategic objective. That is not to say you won't be involved. You will definitely be signing off on the plan and making certain key decisions, but those accountable for action should feel empowered to be creative and get on with delivery as they see fit. Jump to the next chapter to find out how to make sure you delegate effectively and set people up for success.

Hold a Strategic Planning Day

To ensure you have the best possible strategic priorities and have the best chance of achieving buy-in from your team, you need to involve them in the process.

- Get the team together
- Present the strategic objectives you have come up with in conjunction with your senior team, key stakeholders, and boss (as relevant)
- Solicit feedback on each objective
- Open it up to the team to think through further objectives
    - Split them into small teams (if needed) and let them work on ideas for 30 minutes or so
- Get the team(s) to feedback
- Review the ideas and how they match to the strategic objectives you presented – there will be overlap so group them together – they may well build on your initial objective and improve it
- Debate whether any original ideas that have been generated are worth adding as a replacement or as an additional

objective

- o Remember you don't want an exhaustive list. Priority is the key word.
- You now have your final list of strategic priorities expressed as objectives
- Next think about ownership for each objective that you have now decided on
- To ensure ownership you can ask for people to volunteer, you can assign where it is obvious, or you could ask the group who they think would best to lead a particular objective.
  - o The main thing is that the person leading the delivery of the objective is the right person and is motivated to own it
- Assign some people to help each lead person and get them to work through the objective to come up with an initial very top line execution plan and to raise any initial questions they may have.
  - o What are the key milestones and sub-objectives
  - o What resources and budget do they need
  - o What is the time plan
  - o What risks or threats do they envisage
  - o What support do they need from the team and you as the leader
  - o How confident are they in hitting the objective
- They can present this to the group
- After presenting to the group and receiving feedback the execution leads can take this away as their project, which they own.

Execution

"Strategy is a commodity. Execution is an art"

Peter Drucker

After the meeting your role is to ensure there is a tight and clear brief for each strategic objective. With a clear set of expectations and success criteria on which to make decisions.

The execution lead for each objective should agree an execution project team to help deliver the strategic priority.

The execution lead should meet with their execution project team and come back to you within a week or two with:

- a more detailed plan,
- a set of actions
- success criteria and measurement
- any resource requests or questions

Once agreed, you can get out of the way and empower each lead to deliver the strategic priority in the way they see best given the clear direction and accountability they now have.

You can do this with confidence if you have created the right culture and environment for your team following The Empowering Leadership model.

During the execution phase your role is to help unlock resource, support, motivate, and keep momentum behind each project through regular contact and coaching with the execution leads. You will need to help determine and agree changes in the execution plan as needed, in response to changes in the market, competition, budgets, or when things are not working as anticipated.

Your door should be open, and you should be coaching project leads as required using a coaching approach (see Chapter 8) to develop their ability and skills.

Remember as leader you are ultimately accountable for all of these projects; you can delegate responsibility but not completely delegate accountability. You have to be kept up to date and informed during the execution phase.

The best way to ensure you can keep across all projects and know what is going on is to deliver on all parts of The Empowering Leadership model. That is to say build a culture and way of working that means you hear about bad news early, that people know they can tell you the truth and that they are not afraid to speak up. And that you have people with the ability to work autonomously, to make decisions and be agile.

Decision Making

Without decisions we can't move forward, we can't make progress, we stagnate.

If you decide to do something, you may or may not be successful. If you make the wrong decision then things will not go the way you planned, sometimes it will be better than your plan, other times worse. But what is for sure is that if you don't decide, you will not act and therefore you will not be successful.

There are many examples of businesses caught in the trap of indecisiveness often due to the real fear of making a decision that will negatively affect their core business, even when the evidence starts to stack up to show that they need to act, they are sometimes paralysed by indecisiveness and an inability to take a decision to act. Choosing not to do anything.

Take the case of Kodak, the photographic camera and film business that was once synonymous with film and photography in the US, and the UK. *Their marketing slogan "a Kodak moment" even became an everyday expression among Americans, used to describe a meaningful or important experience. Founded in New York in the 1880s, by the 1970s, it held 90% of the film market and 85% of camera sales in the US.*

In 1975, Kodak was the first company to invent the digital camera. Kodak knew that this idea would completely revolutionize photography and that it had the potential to kill the photographic film industry that they dominated. Kodak needed to decide whether or not to act on their new invention, or hold back, for fear of cannibalising their film and paper sales from which they made so much profit.

Despite investing 10s of millions of dollars into the development of the first digital camera, executives within the company decided to drop the product due to fear that introducing the digital camera would threaten their film photography sales. Kodak decided to develop a digital technology strategy in the early 1990s, but even then, it was never fully executed due to a lack of decisiveness and vision by the then executives. Kodak failed to take decisive action to develop digital cameras and failed to execute their digital strategy, so they did not diversify more generally. Fujifilm a very similar Japanese business diversified more successfully during this time. Kodak however fell behind in the market and by 2007 it was 4th in the US behind brands such as Sony, Canon, and Nikon. Then smartphones and tablets began to replace digital cameras in the late-2000s and by 2012, Kodak filed for bankruptcy.

The best way to approach decision making is with a realistic optimism. Optimism and positivity are important aspects of having a growth mindset and can-do drive. But there is an important distinction to make between blind optimism and realistic optimism. Being overly positive and optimistic can lead to a certain degree of fatalism, which can lead to a lack of effort or lack of focus on the importance of one's own actions and agency in delivering the best possible outcome.

As Heidi Grant, Ph.D., explains in the Harvard Business Review (2021). "Realistic optimists... believe they will succeed, but also believe they have to make success happen—through things like effort, careful planning, persistence, and choosing the right strategies." She stresses the importance of thinking about potential hurdles and pitfalls. "They recognize the need for giving serious thought to how they will deal with obstacles. This preparation only increases their confidence in their own ability to get things done."

This type of thinking is often referred to as the Stockdale Paradox, named after James Stockdale, a high-ranking naval officer, who was a Vietnam Prisoner of War for several years. The paradox is in essence an explanation of expecting the best but planning for the worst. It combines facing into the current situation, and appreciating that it may be very difficult, whilst at the same time holding on to the believe that a positive outcome is still possible. It therefore describes a mindset of balancing optimism with realism, even in extremely challenging situations.

Viewing the world through a lens of realistic optimism allows you to be more agile and deal with the inevitable bumps in the road and external influences that can derail or force you to adapt. Thinking about these in advance as will enable you to plan the necessary resource, skills, and training etc that are required.

This ability to balance optimism with realism is one of the features of effective leadership and resilience. Being decisive is an important part of leadership. It is a difficult job sometimes, when faced with big decisions that have potential implications for people, the financial health and / or reputation of the company. Getting comfortable with making decisions and living with your choice is a key challenge of leadership.

Procrastination and Second Guessing

Many people suffer from procrastination and second guessing their decisions once they have made them. Some find it difficult to land on a decision and when they do, they second guess themselves and challenge the decision they made, playing it back and thinking of all the alternatives, beating themselves up if they don't get the decision exactly right.

You may recognise some of these traits in yourself. I know I did for many years. It makes it difficult to be an effective decision maker and therefore leader if you are a procrastinator and if you second guess your every decision.

There is a close correlation between perfectionists and people who find it difficult to make decisions and there is also a correlation to the traits of having fixed mindset, as opposed to a growth mindset (Chapter 4).

Perfectionists by definition are aiming for perfect decisions and this can lead to procrastination and an overload of data as they strive to find out as much as they can in order to make the perfect decision before acting. There comes a point where you will reach information overload and it actually becomes harder to decide as you are overwhelmed by data.

Realising that not only do you not need to make the perfect decision, but in fact you cannot ever make the perfect decision is a key step in starting to shrug off the obsession with perfection.

Developing a growth mindset teaches us that being right all the time is not a goal we should be striving for and that being wrong is a learning experience from which we can grow. Being wrong is a great fear of perfectionists because they feel that if they do not get it "right" and things do not go exactly as they expect, then have failed in some way, and they turn their disappointment on themselves. No one will be as harsh on a perfectionist as they are on themselves when they believe they have made a mistake or things have gone wrong. As a reformed perfectionist (most of the time) I should know!

Being able to make decisions under time pressure and with a limited amount of information is something that leaders are required to do.

Rather than strive for perfection or the "right" decision you need to be looking for the best decision you can make at the time you make it, given the circumstances and the data available. Speed of decision making is often more critical than accuracy, if you miss an opportunity because you are taking too long to decide the accuracy of your decision is academic. You have missed the boat. So, gather as much data and alternatives as you can in the time you have and decide based on what you have and your appetite for and the company's ability to cope with risk.

What you do need to ensure is that you own the decision and know that you did your best at the time with the information and time available. If things don't go to plan, then we learn and we move forward with the knowledge gained.

Self-Awareness

As discussed in Chapter 4, the first step to moving forward in developing your mindset and behaviour is self-awareness. If you become consciously aware that you procrastinate or that you are a perfectionist, you can start to do something about it. Using some of the steps outlined here will help you make better decisions, but it won't help you make perfect decisions (because they don't exist). Professional coaching from a qualified coach can help you work on changing your mindset and support you in improving your decision-making ability.

As part of building your self-awareness ask yourself "How do I make decisions?"

- Do I give sufficient time and thought to bigger or more important decisions?
- Do I rely too much on my gut or intuition even when I don't

have prior knowledge and experience?

- Do I want to have too much information and struggle to decide?
- Do I second guess myself and focus on potential negative outcomes?
- Do I use different approaches for different types of decisions?
- Do I involve enough people in challenging and debating decisions before I decide?
- What biases do I have and how can I become conscious of them?

Agile and Responsive

The best leaders make decisions supported by others' opinions and knowledge, as well as information and insight. They don't look for perfection, they don't second guess themselves, and they are flexible in the face of new information. They are agile enough to change course if their decision turns out to be incorrect or the situation around them changes.

Being agile and responsive in decision making is a strength but you should make changes to your decisions based on the belief that it is the better course of action not simply because some people disagree with you or have criticised your decision.

Circumstances change, the world is extremely fast moving and fluid so as a leader we need to be responsive, there is a difference between staying the course and being stubborn in the face of new data and evidence contrary to your original decision. Keep in mind that once a decision is made you can't just sit back and expect that decision to hold forever, keeping abreast of the market, the economy, technology, competitors and importantly your customers is critical in the execution of strategic decisions.

Being decisive as a leader means that people know that you will act, that you will drive forward momentum and that will get things done. They are likely to respect you as someone who can get things done. Remember a strategy or plan is simply words until you make the decisions necessary to put them into action and that success is born from action.

Not All Decisions are Created Equal

Part of being an effective decision maker is being able to assess the importance and consequence of your decisions. You need to develop the ability to prioritise decision making as you do with tasks. Decision making expends energy and time, you can't spend the same time and energy on every decision.

In fact, you can delegate a lot of decision making as well as tasks, we cover delegation in the next chapter. Don't feel like you have to make every decision that is brought to you. Use coaching techniques (covered in Chapter 8) to help the person bringing the decision to you to reach their own conclusion. In this way they can build up their decision-making confidence and when combined with experience, they will be able to make more decisions for their areas of responsibility.

A lot of decisions will be easy to prioritise and with experience, or the experience of trusted others, you will be able to intuitively prioritise decisions and delegate them when appropriate.

Where decisions are new to you or the team / organisation, or where they have significant consequences then you will need to go through a more formal process.

The type of process and the steps you go through, in reality, will vary depending on how much time pressure you are under, your level of experience, the level of ambiguity and the governance framework you are operating under.

The first step is to assess the situation and the consequences of the decision. When assessing consequences, we need to think about a number of factors:

- What level of complexity are we dealing with?
- What are the financial consequences?
- What are the people consequences?
- What are the reputational consequences?
- What are the ethical and compliance considerations?
- What is the level of risk?
- What is the potential upside?
- How quickly and easily is it to change or alter course?

Time constraints and the available information and insight are also critical factors. Up front you need to be clear on knowing:

- How much time do I have?
- How much information, data and insight can I gather in that time?

These two questions really determine what decision-making options are open to you. If you have a number of weeks then things like extensive research, brainstorming sessions, modelling scenarios and war gaming are all open to you.

If you need to make the decision more quickly you may have to make the decision with incomplete information, with limited input and limited opportunity to test scenarios.

Some of the questions to ask yourself are:

- Does this need to be a collaborative decision with my team and/or key stakeholders?
- What information and insight can I get in the time available?
- Who can I include in helping make the decision?
- How do I ensure a diverse range of input?
- How do I account for bias?
- Have I explored all possible solutions in the time available?
- What's ideal outcome and how much compromise am I willing to make?
- Do we have the capability and capacity – (people and resources) to action the decision?
- Are there previous decisions that I can learn from?

Making Better Decisions

Objectives and Decision Criteria

First, we should set clear objectives and success criteria to judge our decisions against before looking for possible solutions and alternatives. This is the same as asking, "what does success look like?".

Setting your decision criteria up front will prevent you from having an idea of what you want and then setting your criteria to match what you already think. This can lead you into the trap of confirmation bias. This is when we want to believe a position is the right one and then we look for information that supports it and filter out or actively avoid information or opinions we think may derail or contradict our initial preferred position.

Always check your options against your decision criteria and objectives to avoid deciding on something contrary to your success criteria, either through pressure from others or due to unconscious bias.

Find the alternatives

What research shows is that decision making most often falls down because people fail to generate alternative options. One research study finding that no alternative idea generation occurred in 85% of the decisions studied (Nutt, 1994), thus leading to decision makers focusing in on a preferred choice, and succumbing to confirmation bias, where they look for information and feedback that confirms their initial choice.

Being open to alternative ideas, suggestions and even to thinking about a completely different direction than you initially had in mind, can greatly enhance the quality of decision making. If you adopt a growth and learning mindset you will be curious and inquisitive about the alternatives.

But we should not be looking for too many alternatives, there needs to be sensible limit based on how closely the alternatives have the potential to meet your success criteria and objectives. Too many options can lead to confusion, so a balance needs to be struck between considering every possible alternative and several realistic alternatives as measured against their potential to meet the objectives and success criteria.

Too much information can lead to paralysis, where more and more time is spent on analysing and thinking about it, but a decision does not get made. As mentioned above perfectionists can end up with too much information as they search for the perfect solution, ending up with information overload.

Ask yourself what would more data or information add to the decision-making process? Would it improve the certainty or outcome?

Will it tell me anything I don't know?

Do I really need any more information for the decision in front of me?

The beauty of having decision criteria up front is you can confidently assess a course of action against them. If you have a solution that satisfies all of your decision criteria, do you need to spend any longer or gather any more data?

Note that if you are using a brainstorming type of exercise to generate alternatives, which is a good option, by the end of the process you need to come back to the 3 or 4 alternatives by filtering the ideas through the funnel of your decision criteria and objectives.

Seek Diverse Opinions and Discussion

Disagreement and discussion can lead to more rational strategic decisions by ensuring they are fully tested. This is best done by proactively seeking a diverse range of views and opinions. Not just from your peers or the most experienced. Soliciting views from people outside your functional area or from younger / less experienced people can give you a fresh perspective. The naive questions that come from a place of no baggage, no history and no vested interest will often lead to lateral thinking and fresh perspectives.

Again, you have to be in a growth and learning mindset, open and confident to fresh perspectives without being defensive to your initial thoughts and position. By all means defend your final decision to help get it accepted and actioned, but during the decision-making process being open is good.

Finding alternatives, proactively seeking input and alternative opinions limits the chance of becoming a victim of confirmation bias. It is impossible to rule out bias completely but the steps I am recommending here can help limit its impact. So don't limit yourself to asking people who you think will agree with you and support you, make sure you test your idea and challenge confirmation bias.

Look At Existing Solutions to Similar Problems

Learning from others is always a good thing, in fact many business leaders will tell you that it is a critical part of being successful.

Sam Walton the founder of Walmart famously said, "Most everything I've done, I've copied from somebody else." And Steve Jobs was a fan of quoting Picasso who said, "Good artists' copy. Great artists Steal"

So, when making decisions it is good to look for learning from other's decisions, that you may be able to apply to your own situation. But be careful about simply copying a course of action, particularly when dealing with complex decisions.

Another bias can kick in here which is, survivorship bias, this can cause us to make decisions based only on examples of success, assuming that we have the full story and that this is a model for all similar decisions in similar circumstances. The problem is that Company X may well have been very successful with the strategy they have pursued, but firstly it was a unique set of circumstances for them and secondly what people often don't consider are the other companies who tried the same strategy and failed.

The successful outcomes of a decision made by another company will have had a specific set of complex circumstances and particular criteria in place at the time that led to the decision being successful. It's important to take the learnings you can, but equally important not to assume that you can just follow the decision and expect the same results.

To avoid survivorship bias, train yourself to be more sceptical, and question what particular circumstances led to that success, question the success myth of a business that is always developed in hindsight as part of their marketing story. Challenge yourself honestly as to whether you really could be as successful with the same strategy given your specific set of internal and external circumstances, resources, talent, and your products or services.

Consider a Range of Outcomes

Considering your decision as a range of outcomes will help you check your decision still makes sense across a range of possible results. It will give you an idea of how robust your decision is and what the risk tolerance is.

You can consider a range of financial outcomes for example and ask yourself if a realistic worst-case scenario were to happen what does the financial impact look like and can you live with it.

Conversely if you get a realistic level of upside do you have the capacity available to match the upside. This leads to scenario planning which can guide final decision making based on risk tolerance and growth potential.

Have a range of scenarios shows that you are being realistic about the possible outcomes, and it gives you the opportunity to check risk and upside. You can take a view on whether the decision is still a good one and if you do go ahead, you can have plans to mitigate a realistic level of risk and plans to provide resources for a realistic level of upside.

Growing too quickly can be as much of an issue for a business as not growing as quickly as you expected. Growing too quickly can threaten cash flow, customer service, product quality, quality of recruitment and even your culture.

Peloton the upmarket home exercise company based on spin bikes and treadmills has suffered from growing too quickly. In 2020 during the Covid pandemic they had amazing growth in subscribers, revenue and share price. In early 2021, Peloton continued its growth, due to sustained demand for in-home fitness as the pandemic carried on.

They invested heavily in production and supply chain to keep up with demand and based on the assumption it would continue to grow. However, as people started going back to the gym and fitness studios post Covid restrictions Peloton sales took a sharp decline. Product quality and service also suffered during this period of rapid growth as they cut corners desperately trying to keep up with demand, damaging the *reputation of the brand. The company's stock dropped 34% following an earnings report in November 2021, which included a poor outlook for the months ahead. By January 2022 they had to stop production of new equipment, as they had huge excess stock and halt plans to build $400 million factory.*

The CEO then stepped down and announced that the company was cutting 2,800 jobs, about 20% of its workforce, and with further cuts through 2022 bringing the total to around 5,200 jobs. As the departing CEO commented "We've made missteps along the way. To meet market demand, we scaled our operations too rapidly. And we overinvested in certain areas of our business". (businessinsider.com)

Communication

Communication throughout decision making is a key part of setting yourself up for success in terms of being able to put your decisions into action.

You should be thinking about communication from the start of your decision-making process. Asking yourself:

- Who does this decision affect directly?
- Who does it affect indirectly?
- When do I need to communicate to each stakeholder?
- What do I need to communicate to each stakeholder?

You can think about this stage of the process as working out:

- Who needs to be consulted on the decision, so that they can input into the thinking
- Who needs to be informed about the decision, not just the final decision but also at various stages throughout the process.

I spent a lot of my career in leadership roles at the centre of matrix organisations providing a service for a number of divisions, each with their own managing executive. Leading a group function with resources shared by multiple leaders meant having to consider the needs and objectives of multiple executive stakeholders. The only way I could successfully action change and create forward momentum was through effective communication. I learned through success and failure about the importance of knowing who to consult and who to inform, and how to communicate to different individuals.

Not communicating even, a relatively small change can cause big ramifications so always remember to think about who needs to be involved and who needs to know what is going on.

Your Objectives and Actions from this Chapter

- Give your team clear direction through strategic priorities
- Set shared strategic objectives that your team buys into
- Assign ownership to each objective
- Empower, coach, and support the team to execute the strategic objectives
- Develop self-awareness about your decision-making patterns and your attitude to decision making

- Prioritise your decision-making approach
- Establish your decision / success criteria to judge alternatives by
- Consider alternatives, seek diverse opinions, encourage discussion
- Look for learnings from existing solutions to similar problems with a sceptical eye
- Plan for a number of scenarios by considering a range of outcomes to your decision
- Think about your communication plan throughout the decision making process – who to consult and who to inform and when.

7. Principle 4 - Delegate, Empower, Trust

> "People and organizations don't grow
> much without delegation."
>
> *(Stephen R. Covey)*

My aim in this book is to provide practical, straightforward ways of applying the lessons from each chapter so that you have a how to guide you can use in your organisation with your team.

If you are going to get the most out of people and maximise their potential, you have be willing and able to let them get on with it.

- You need to empower and support them to do their best, make decisions and deliver results.
- You need to be able to trust them to come to you when they need to. They need to trust that you will be there for them.
- You cannot empower people if you don't provide the coaching, training, resources, and support structure they need.
- You cannot delegate effectively if you don't very clearly define roles, responsibilities, and objectives. Making it clear what your expectations are and what people are expected to do and to deliver.
- You cannot delegate or empower if you don't fundamentally trust your people to deliver.

Why We Find It Difficult to Delegate

"The inability to delegate is one of the
biggest problems I see with managers
at all levels."

(Eli Broad)

Delegation is something many managers and leaders struggle with it is often one of the hardest things for a new manager to let go and to trust someone else to do it. Let's unpack the reasons why it is so difficult for many people to delegate before we get on to how to delegate effectively.

At the root of people's reluctance to delegate lie three emotions of control, fear and trust and a practical element of time and efficiency.

People don't want to delegate because of trust and / or fear:

- They don't trust the person to do the job they need doing
- They fear losing control of the process and output,
- They fear the consequences of things going wrong, mistakes being made, or deadlines being missed
- They fear it not being done in exactly the same way they would have done it!

The final element that puts people off delegating is the view that it takes longer than doing it yourself, by the time you have explained what you want and how do to it you feel you could have done it better yourself and therefore what's the point.

Some people might say, "I haven't got time to delegate, I have to explain everything, support them and deal with the questions, it's just quicker and easier to do it myself, and I get it the way I would always do it."

Not delegating because of these reasons is ignoring the adage, "Give a man a fish and it will feed him for a day, teach a man to fish and it will feed him for a lifetime." Not delegating saves you a short-term headache, but it does nothing to help you long term and it teaches nothing to the person you could delegate to.

Delegating properly does take time but you have to think of it as a long-term investment that will pay dividends for years to come. Getting over the fear of losing control and of negative consequences can be achieved by delegating effectively.

If you take the time to invest in delegating responsibility and tasks effectively then you enable and support people to deliver the delegated task, you drastically reduce the fears that hold you back. You may still feel nervous and fearful, but it should be tempered by the fact you know you have delegated effectively and that you are supporting them.

The more successful outcomes you have then the less fearful you will become and the easier it gets to let go and hand over control and responsibility, but importantly not full accountability... more on this shortly.

Definitions

Effective Delegation is empowering, trusting, and enabling someone to take responsibility for the delivery of a task or project, with minimal supervision safe in the knowledge they have the capacity, capability and support needed to succeed.

Empowering and enabling are two sides of the same coin, you cannot effectively empower someone without enabling them to do their job to the best of their ability.

Empowering means giving someone the responsibility to make decisions to deliver something with the necessary support. It means giving them freedom to get on with it, but it does not include a full transfer of accountability.

You can make someone fully responsible, but you have to maintain shared accountability. The buck stops with you, you are ultimately accountable for your team and their performance. Unlike certain politicians (mentioning no names) you cannot say you are not accountable when something goes wrong. With the proviso that the person you delegated to works under the normal ethical, procedural, and regulatory norms of your company and industry and is not negligent in anyway.

If you own this idea of joint accountability, you will delegate much more effectively because you are jointly accountable for the success or failure. You will do all you can to fully enable them to succeed.

Importantly empowering people is not just handing things over without the support, training, resources, and guidance required. To properly empower you also need to enable people to succeed.

Enabling means giving people the knowledge, skills, resources, tools and support they need to be successful, including coaching, access to resources and networks, guidance, and training.

If you have effectively enabled the delegated person, it makes it easier to trust them and impart them with the responsibility because you are confident, they have what it takes, and they have the resources and support they need.

Meaningful feedback throughout the process is also an integral part of effective delegation. Ensuring that you receive feedback regularly and you provide useful and targeted feedback that is timely, forward looking and focused on delivering performance benefits (see Chapter 8 for more on feedback).

The Critical Components

1. Capacity and Capability

Firstly, you need to be sure that the person has the capability and capacity, to be empowered with a specific task.

Capacity refers to an individual's ability to absorb change or take on new tasks effectively. People can only take on a certain amount of new knowledge, tasks or change before they become overloaded, the consequences of which may include, underperformance, burnout, depression, or anxiety.

- Capacity is a finite resource. Think of capacity like a single bucket. Once its full you need to stop adding to it otherwise it will overflow.
- Capacity is a singular resource that is not divided between work and personal lives. In other words, your team members' capacity might be being taken up with personal stuff (bereavement, moving home, illness, financial struggles etc) or they may have a busy period at work due to a project, or they may have just taken on a new job in a new company. Therefore, they may not have sufficient capacity left to take on more new responsibilities, tasks, or knowledge at a point

in time.

The goal, then, is to build awareness of the capacity of your team members and to know enough about them through your relationship so that you have some understanding of how they may react to change or stretch objectives. They should also feel comfortable to raise any issues around capacity, without fear of retribution in an emotionally safe environment.

Capacity can be built over time through experience, by building resilience and coping mechanisms so that the finite amount of capacity a person has increases and therefore people can take on more and assimilate greater amounts of change, but it will always be finite.

We can help build capacity and support people who are at their limit by doing the following.

- Providing more time, if possible, to complete a task in order to allow for their workload or the amount of new assimilation required.
- Give additional resource or delegate tasks to someone else to help reduce their workload and give them the head space to take on new responsibilities
- Providing a culture of support and emotional safety by demonstrating understanding that change and learning something new is difficult. They can ask for help and flag genuine mistakes or delays without fear.
- Finally, when delegating new responsibilities, you can support by giving encouragement to boost resilience and energy levels to complete the tasks.

Capability refers to the skills and knowledge required for a particular task. A person may have the capacity to change, but lack certain key capabilities, which you can build to ensure they have the ability and confidence to take on the task.

The solution to gaps in capability is to provide the appropriate training and coaching, knowledge transfer and ongoing technical support. It is important to be aware of the capability of the person before delegating responsibility for a task.

Bear in mind that a lot of the necessary experience and knowledge comes on the job, which is where ongoing coaching and mentoring support are a crucial ingredient to effective delegation and true empowerment. This is coaching provided by you as a leader, another mentor in the workplace or sometimes through a professional coach.

There is a correlation between the concepts of capacity and capability building. In many cases, building capability by increasing a person's knowledge, experience and skills can actually help expand their capacity as you can give them more tools and mechanisms to cope.

This is what we want to achieve by effective delegation, empowerment, and support. We want to build capabilities through experience, coaching, training, and guidance so that we in turn build capacity in the person to take on more. This is the essence of working smarter, not harder, by giving people the tools, ability, and capacity to deal with new tasks and change more effectively and efficiently.

2. How You Delegate

Always be clear on the What, Why, When and How.

1. What it is you are delegating
2. Why you need it doing
3. When it needs to be completed by
4. How you want the work to be completed

The What needs to be as clear as possible

When delegating you need to allow for questions and challenge. Even if what you are delegating is broad and somewhat ambiguous you need to break it down to ensure you can give clarity about what your desired outcome or objective is.

Setting clear objectives is critical to good delegation and the way to do this is best viewed using a set of principles. I use Lock and Latham's 5 principles as a check list for determining an objective.

Lock and Latham's 5 principles work well, and I believe it offers a set of guiding principles against which to check that the objectives you are setting are well structured, easy to understand and follow, have the buy in of the person being delegated to and includes the all-important feedback loop. The first three steps are concerned with how you set the objective and the last two steps relate to how you help with its implementation and follow through.

The five principles are:

1. Complexity – break down into the least complex steps

2. Clarity – Clear, unambiguous, and precise

3. Challenge – the sweet spot of stretching but achievable

4. Commitment – check and recheck commitment to goal

5. Feedback – progress feedback and course correction

Applying these principles, even to more complex areas of learning or performance, helps to ensure that the objective for the delegated task is something that can be achieved and measured, i.e., we'll know when it's done.

A good example of how these principles can help derive useful objectives even with complex and ambiguous objectives is the area of behavioural development.

Many of you will have had a boss say to you in a performance review something like "you need to be more assertive," or, "you need to have more impact," or "you need to influence more effectively".

All of these are important, valid, and common aspects of behavioural development but it's difficult for the person being told these things to do anything about it, without it been broken down into individual components that can be acted upon by the person receiving the objective.

This is the first step, reduce complexity and focus on individual aspects of the broader goal. Once this is achieved it is easier to agree clear and precise objectives for the constituent parts. For example, instead of "you need to have more impact" being the statement and the person being expected to do something with it, we can break this down to a first objective of:

"You should ask one question and make at least one comment in every meeting."

This is simple, clear, and even if it is a challenge for a particular individual, achievable. It is something they can commit to as it is easy to understand, and feedback can be given on this first step easily as they build their confidence, presence, and impact.

In setting the goal you should ensure that you are open to challenge from the person you are delegating to. You should be creating a culture and a relationship with your team members that makes them feel comfortable to question, challenge, and to propose alternatives. This leads to better decisions and a better brief for the person delegated to (see more on decision making in Chapter 6). It also increases buy in and helps reinforce commitment.

What about SMART objectives?

SMART is clearly a very successful and widely used model, that has its place. Personally I often struggled to fit my objectives consistently and successfully into the SMART model, particularly broad-based strategic objectives or objectives that are long term and multifaceted. I feel like the SMART construct can become a straitjacket that forces all goals into the same model. I found it time consuming and inefficient when attempting to crowbar all of my objectives into it. In my opinion a model should not be an end itself but rather merely a tool to help you do the best job you can.

A set of principles, like Lock and Latham's 5 principles, gives you much more flexibility and room to set objectives in a way that suits the task and that suits your communication and writing style.

The Why is critical to effective delegation

Real commitment and buy-in is only possible if people understand the why. People want to feel their job and their effort is part of something bigger, that they are adding value and they want to understand how their work fits into achieving the team or company goals.

Motivation is driven much more by the why than the what. People are motivated by a sense of purpose and an inner belief that what they are doing matters beyond the task itself. You need to be able to explain how the task you are delegating is going to help the team achieve its goals, why it matters in the greater scheme of things and what the benefits are.

Even mundane tasks need to be set in context, you may not be able to truly motivate and inspire with every task you delegate (let's be real about it) but you can always explain how it helps you, the team, or the company. It may help in a tangential way by freeing up your time to complete something else, attend an important meeting or because the task is part of a bigger project with clear benefits.

When leading teams, I would rarely just ask (never tell) any of my team to do something, I didn't buy into JFDI because it doesn't motivate people. Even when delegating mundane, simple, and relatively unimportant tasks I would always explain how it would help (what the benefits are), and why it is important.

Alternative examples of how you could delegate a relatively simple task:

"I need you to complete this spreadsheet for me every week to log the instances of invoice error that we are

experiencing. *It's important it gets done every week by Friday at 1 pm and sent to me for review and inclusion in my report. I appreciate your help on this one. Let me know if you have any questions"*

This is not bad. A lot of managers will be worse. But alternatively, you could explain the importance of this relatively simple and mundane task and the benefits it can help deliver.

"One of our team objectives this year is to reduce the number of invoice errors to improve our customer service and reduce costs within the business, it is part of the wider company initiative to improve efficiency and reduce costs.

To be able get on top of the issue we need to know the scale of the problem and be able to analyse the data to look for patterns; without this we won't be able to achieve our objective so it's really important we gather this data.

In order to help with this, I need you to complete this spreadsheet for me every week to log the instances of invoice error that we are experiencing. It's important it gets done every week by Friday at 1 pm and sent to me for review and inclusion in my report.

I'd value your input into the process and spreadsheet layout, as well as any insight you can glean from the data, which would be invaluable. Do you have any questions or suggestions at this point?"

We can see from this example that the explanation of why and the benefits obtained from the work would greatly improve the chance of commitment and sense of motivation to complete the task. There is no dressing up of the delegated task, but it is clear that without this work being completed properly an important team and company objective will not be achievable, therefore it is of import and meaningful work.

Be clear and transparent about When you need the work

We all know plans change and timings change. Being honest, transparent, and straight forward about timings is another key determining factor of the level of motivation of the person delegated to.

It is frustrating and demotivating when the person who delegates you a task messes around with the timing, it makes you feel like your time is not important and that they are taking you for granted. The opposite feelings we want to inspire in a motivated team member.

- We have all experienced the boss who pads lots of time into the deadline for themselves, putting you under pressure only for them to sit on your work for a couple of weeks before they get back to you or use it themselves.
- We've all had instances where the timing is not clear because the person delegating was fuzzy and then all of a sudden you have "missed" a deadline that no one has communicated to you.
- Some things are genuinely urgent, but we've all had the frustration of a boss where everything is urgent because they can't get their stuff together to organise themselves and delegate in a timely manner.

None of these situations are motivational for the person being delegated to. If they happen regularly, they can cause frustration, resentment, poor work, and disengaged employees.

- Always give a deadline even if you are relaxed about when you get something back. People need to plan their work into their schedule, and you have to respect their time.
- Be up front and honest about your timing. Tell the truth and trust your people to work with you on it.
- Tell them the deadline and explain why you need the work from them a week before (or however long a lead time you need)
- Make sure you acknowledge the work when it comes to you even if you are not going to get to it or use it right away
- If something is urgent, and important, then give a very clear deadline and explain why it's urgent
- Plan your delegation so that you can avoid everything being urgent. The best thing to do is delegate as soon as you are aware of the fact you need something doing

You should be creating a culture and relationships that enable your team members to ask you if the deadline is still the same, to suggest new deadlines based on their workload and to feel like they can communicate with you as needed. Remember that we should be prioritising our own work into important non urgent and important urgent.

MANAGE & DELEGATE	STRATEGIC FOCUS
Pressing Priorities & Problems	Medium & Long Term Goals, Values & People
KEY PRIORITIES DAILY FIREFIGHTING EFFECTIVE DELEGATION	CREATE AND INNOVATE OPPS AND THREATS PEOPLE DEVELOPMENT
Important And Urgent	**Important Not Urgent**
AVOID	MINIMISE
Busy Work & Distractions	Trivial & Guilty Pleasures
LEARN TO IDENTIFY NOT YOUR PROBLEM IGNORE OR DO LATER	LIMIT TO NEED STRESS RELIEF BUILD RELATIONSHIPS
Urgent Not Important	**Not Urgent / Important**

How you want the work to be completed

Beware the perfectionist and micro manager, this is not an invitation for you to tell people exactly how to do something! We want to empower people to do things their way, but we may have some requirements around the format, layout or specific regulations or professional guidelines. It's important to specify this up front. Remember the more you can provide clarity upfront the better things will go and the more trust you can have in the person you delegate to.

Now get out of the way!

So, you followed the advice contained in this chapter and you have successfully delegated the task, explained why it's important and what the benefits are, you set a clear deadline and explained how you want the work completed. You should now let the person get on with it.

3. Empower

The person delegated to needs to own the task fully and have full responsibility for its delivery.

- You have to feel comfortable letting go and letting them get on with it, so that they can exercise their ownership.
- You have to trust them to come to you when they need a question answered, additional resource, guidance, or support.
- You have to trust in your effective delegation that they know what to do, why they are doing it and how to do it.
- Avoid the temptation to jump in and give all the answers at the first sign of trouble but rather use coaching (Chapter 8) so that they maintain ownership and responsibility.

Responsibility in a business context can be defined as someone's duty to perform or complete a task. Accountability is an assurance that an individual or an organization will be held to account and be evaluated on their performance of something for which they are responsible.

Whilst they are fully responsible for the delivery of the delegated task you have to maintain shared accountability. This means you are still ultimately accountable for the work and the delivery of the team members and the team overall. Shared accountability is an important precept in delegation as your team member needs to feel they will not be hung out to dry! Clearly the assumption is that the person delegated to works with in the normal ethical boundaries and is transparent with you about how things are going, flags mistakes and delays or problems early and openly and is not knowingly negligent in anyway.

4. Enabling

This is the foundation of being able to get out of the way, delegate effectively and truly empower your team to become self-managed and highly effective. Enabling has a number of elements related to the support and framework that exists in your team to support empowerment. This includes giving people the knowledge, skills, and tools they need to be successful, including coaching, access to resources and networks, guidance, and training.

It also includes creating the right culture with high levels of emotional safety (see Chapter 9 for more on this) and a growth mindset (Chapter 4) to ensure that people feel safe and secure in their ability to flag bad news early, highlight delays and mistakes and call out any practices that are hindering their progress or threaten safety or integrity.

If we enable people to take ownership and responsibility in the full knowledge of why they are doing their job and with clear expectations established in an environment where managers and leaders are empathetic, then you will get highly engaged and highly motivated people giving their best and delivering results.

Your Objectives and Actions from this Chapter

- Understand the capacity and capability of your team members
- Clearly define roles, responsibilities, objectives, and expectations
- Practice Effective Delegation – What, Why, When, How
- Get out of their way and Empower and Support them to own it
- Deliver the environment, culture and resources that Enables them to succeed
- Prioritise your workload so you can delegate the important non urgent stuff ahead of time

8. Principle 5 – Coach for Performance

"Coaching is unlocking people's potential to maximize their own performance. It is more often helping them to learn rather than teaching them."

(John Whitmore)

As a qualified leadership coach, you might expect coaching to be one of the pillars of The Empowering Leadership model, but my belief in a coaching leadership style stems more from my twenty plus years' experience as a leader and from working with other teams and leaders across a range of organisations. I have seen the benefits of this approach in building people's ability, self-belief, and their decision-making capability.

A coaching approach treats people with respect, by giving them the opportunity to be listened to, to clarify their thinking and to commit to self-development thereby increasing their capability. As discussed in Chapter 7, by helping people to increase their capability you can also increase their capacity to take on more change and more responsibility. Ultimately a coaching approach results in improved performance, with people building strong decision-making capabilities, confidence, and a drive to act.

A coaching approach treats people as adults. It is focused on maximising the potential of people and thereby maximising their performance as part of a high performing team. It helps you do this by delivering greater employee engagement, collaboration, meaningful joint goal setting, effective delegation, empowerment, and accountability – all of the things we have covered so far that underpin The Empowering Leadership approach.

The number of studies into the effectiveness of coaching has grown over the past 10 to 15 years but remains relatively small when compared to Psychology for instance. However, there is a body of research into coaching effectiveness as reported by Mackie, who concludes "there is growing evidence for coaching's effectiveness as a methodology for developing skills, abilities and awareness in the workplace." (Mackie, 2016)

And, as the father of performance coaching in the workplace John Whitmore stated about the impact of a coaching leadership style based on over 30 years of experience, "What are the implications for organizations whose leaders adopt a coaching leadership style...? Those leaders will, indisputably, create the conditions for a high-performance culture." (Whitmore, 2017)

Coaching and Mentoring Defined

I am not going to spend too long on coaching and mentoring as professional disciplines, my goal here is not to make you into a professional coach but to give you guidance on using coaching and mentoring techniques as a leader, because I believe these are crucial to developing people, and maximising their potential.

However, by way of introduction and background I want to briefly outline some definitions around coaching and mentoring. My definition, which attempts to cover all of the elements as I see it, is as follows:

Coaching aims to deliver optimal performance at work

by empowering people through facilitation to acquire new knowledge, develop new skills and build new behaviours. It is goal orientated with a focus on setting objectives and identifying actions that deliver improved performance. Coaching does not direct, teach, or tell, but promotes self-discovery through self-directed learning, stimulated by the coach.

The key thing to take from this definition that distinguishes coaching as distinct from mentoring and other kinds of development techniques, is the fact that the coach does not direct, teach, or tell. Mentoring can be defined as:

A professional guiding relationship between a more experienced or senior person and less experienced person, focussed on imparting knowledge, giving advice, and providing direction to help them to acquire new knowledge, develop new skills and build new behaviours that deliver improved performance.

The key take out here is the fact that the mentor guides, directs, gives advice, and imparts knowledge, in contrast to the coach who facilitates and empowers the coachee to discover their own answers.

Coaching and Mentoring are by no means mutually exclusive. The European Mentoring and Coaching Council core competencies for professional coaches and mentors does not distinguish between them. Mentors add to the skills of coaching by using their relevant knowledge and experience more directly, many coaches do not have specific experience or knowledge of the industry or role to impart. Mentors are also more likely to be role models and sounding boards and may help the mentee more directly in answering questions and building networks. (Clutterbuck, 2020)

The Coaching Spectrum

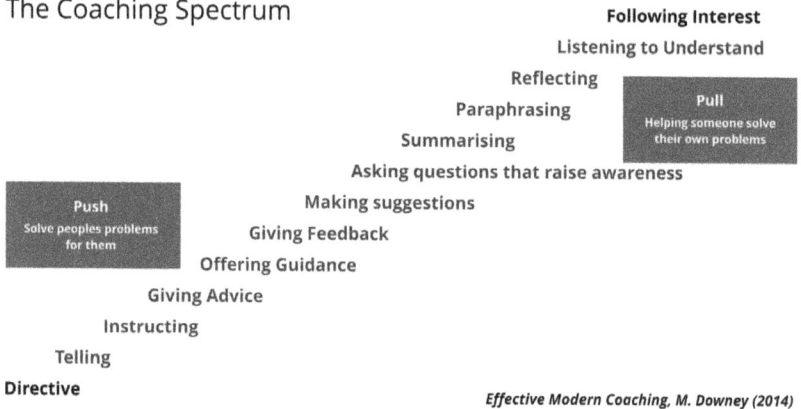

Following Interest
Listening to Understand
Reflecting
Paraphrasing
Summarising

Pull
Helping someone solve
their own problems

Asking questions that raise awareness
Making suggestions

Push
Solve peoples problems
for them

Giving Feedback
Offering Guidance
Giving Advice
Instructing
Telling

Directive

Effective Modern Coaching, M. Downey (2014)

Another way to view coaching and mentoring is to see them as two ends of a spectrum. Miles Downey (2014) has developed a useful spectrum to highlight the types of intervention that can be used in the practice of coaching and mentoring.

In simple terms coaching often aims to be more at the "pull" end of the spectrum, for more of the time, and mentoring more at the middle to the "push" end. In reality effective mentors need to use the skills present at the pull end of the spectrum and some professional coaches may well use their experience to guide and direct, with the permission of the coachee. But coaches generally, avoid giving advice as much as possible, as do some mentors, preferring to guide and facilitate their mentees to reaching their own decision and making their own choices.

Using Coaching and Mentoring as a Leader

Coaching and mentoring as a leadership and development style works because it treats the employee as an adult, it acknowledges their capacity for growth, and it works on building self-belief and self-reliance. Whitmore noted that "Adult learning theory tells us that adults learn in a completely different way to children. Self-belief is central to this. Coaching is adult learning in practice and is both what leaders need and the direction in which leadership style needs to travel. In essence coaching is about partnership, collaboration, and believing in potential." (Whitmore 2017)

When using coaching as the leader of a team a realistic approach is necessary. As a leader who used coaching and mentoring as much as possible, I was aware of the limitations of the "pure" coaching end of the spectrum in a work setting, given the different levels of experience and knowledge faced with and the time pressure we are often under. In practice as a coaching leader, you will be working as a coaching mentor. Where coaching leadership differs from directive leadership is in using instruction only where necessary for urgent tasks for example, for a technical skill or process briefing, and it avoids the use of telling all together.

Telling and demanding without debate or listening to the other person is disrespectful, it cuts out alternatives and choice, it disempowers, demotivates, and fosters a blame dynamic. Coaching and mentoring do the opposite, they empower people and therefore increase engagement and motivation.

I define a coaching leader as:

A leader who employs coaching and mentoring techniques as part of their leadership approach with the intention to develop in others greater self-awareness, knowledge, skills, and behaviours, so that individuals and the team are motivated and able to increase performance.

The coaching process is a learning process for the leader doing the coaching as well as the coachee. Through a respectful dialogue driven approach where listening to understand and asking questions to raise awareness are a fundamental part of the dynamic, both participants will learn. The quality and creativity of solutions found, and decisions made will improve.

Ownership of the decisions made is a natural outcome of the coaching process, because the coachee has been involved in the process and has come to their own conclusion they are more committed to the decision. This means they are more likely to be motivated to take ownership of the decision and be responsible for ensuring it gets actioned, with sufficient resources and support.

Coaching and Mentoring Leadership Skills

I want to now look at the fundamentals of coaching and mentoring that will help you put this style of leadership into practice in your workplace, in a way that fits with day to day working and the demands of a leadership role.

Relationships

The starting point to building engaged and motivated team is to take an interest in them as people, get to know them, build a genuine relationship that goes beyond a hierarchical power-based relationship. This will provide you with the foundation of trust that everything else is built upon.

I am not saying you need to be best buddies with everyone and know all of the intimate details of their life, but in the context of a professional working relationship you need to take an interest in them as people and as individuals. You can't get the best out of people if you don't know what makes them tick, what their strengths, weaknesses and preferences are. And you can't judge their motivators if you don't know what is important to them.

I mentioned in Chapter 4 that it is important to understand what capacity your team member has for taking on new stretch tasks or dealing with change. As a reminder or an introduction if you have jumped to this chapter. Capacity refers to an individual's ability to absorb change or take on new tasks effectively. People can only take on a certain amount of new knowledge, tasks or change before they become overloaded, the consequences of which may include, underperformance, burnout, depression, or anxiety.

Capacity then, is a finite resource. Think of capacity like a single bucket. Once its full you need to stop adding to it otherwise it will overflow. It is a singular resource that is not divided between work and personal lives. In other words, your team members' capacity might be being taken up with personal things as well as their work life, and whilst we can't pry into people's personal lives, we need to be cognisant of the fact and attuned to what's going on. The better the relationship and the more mutual trust exists the better understanding you will have of their capacity at any point in time.

So, firstly take an interest in people. Take time to get to know them and to understand a little about what makes them tick, what they like doing, what they are good at and how they are feeling more generally. It takes time but with respect, trust and a genuine interest in people you will build a more solid foundation for a mutually beneficial relationship.

Whatever you do, don't do what I have witnessed bosses do many times over the years. Which is display faux rapport and interest. Where they ask about how you are or how things are going but immediately glaze over or start to look at their screen/notes when you start to speak. They know the theory, but they don't really buy into it, or perhaps their ego and sense of self-importance is too big to let them really be interested in other people.

You can be building relationships all the time. During the interview stage if you are recruiting, on their first day, brief moments at the coffee station, walking by their desk, in one to ones or at the start of a meeting. It's not going to happen overnight in one big session. Don't force it, just be natural it takes time, show an interest, and treat people with the same respect you expect.

Listening, Reflecting and Questioning

These are the three fundamental activities of a coaching and mentoring style of leadership.

1. Active listening with the intent to understand what is being said
2. Reflecting back what people have said to check understanding and prompt further information
3. Asking open questions to generate insight and self-

awareness

Practicing and becoming competent at all of these will elevate your interactions with your team and you will find that over time you get much more creative thought and idea generation, as well as building skills in your team members that will allow them to be more autonomous and make more decisions themselves.

These are also useful life skills that can help in any kind of interaction. Being a better listener will add value to any situation, including negotiation, meetings, networking and in your personal relationships. Likewise reflecting back through paraphrase or summary can help reduce misunderstandings and draw out more information and asking open questions reduces defensiveness and elicits greater detail.

Listening and Reflecting

As we have seen the power of coaching comes through enabling people to find their own answers and gain insight. When someone comes to you with a problem your first thought may be to give them the answer, maybe you are an expert, or you are in hurry, or you just feel it would be helpful. This may be what is needed but try not to rush into giving advice or solutions, start at the top of the coaching spectrum and help people to think for themselves first.

Most of the time, most of us are not listening to understand if we are honest. Depending on the situation, the person speaking and what's going on in our lives we are usually listening in one of three ways, which I am sure you will recognise.

Firstly, surface listening is where we are not really listening at all, we give the impression we are, or at least attempt to look like we are listening, but we could probably not repeat back much of what we heard.

One of the most common states of listening is conversational listening, this is where we are thinking about our response as the other person is talking, before they have finished their point. Our focus is on ourselves and how clever and insightful we are going to sound or how we can contradict or add to what is being said. This makes us impatient to speak, which we may show through body language, signalling to the other person we are eager for them to finish, or just by interrupting.

In a business setting many people are in critical listening mode, where they are listening, but not neutrally or with the intent to understand, but rather they are critically evaluating every word and deciding their response before the full information has been transmitted. And before they have had chance to really think about how they feel and what they think about the information. Again, there is an impatience to speak building up, which can lead to interruptions before the speaker has finished their thoughts.

Active listening means listening with one's full attention and not thinking about what you are going to say, questions should be spontaneous based purely on what you hear. Active listening also includes reflecting back and clarifying with the speaker to ensure correct understanding and to reinforce that the person is being listened to. As Nancy Kline in her excellent bestseller Time to Think, succinctly defines it, "Listening with respect and without interruption" (1999)

Kline also summarises beautifully the power of listening and being fully present with the phrase, "The quality of your attention determines the quality of other people's thinking" (1999).

If you have ever had the pleasure of someone really listening to you, without interruption, giving you time to think, reflecting back what you have said, you will know that it really helps you think. It allows you to express yourself fully and with confidence. Without the fear of interruption or an immediate critical response you can fully form your thoughts and get across what really mean. Contrast that with the pressure of rushing through your answer in a busy meeting because you know someone will jump in mid-sentence at some point, spoil your flow and interrupt your train of thought.

In my practice as a coach, I have found that the biggest benefit to the coachee is the simple fact of being listened to properly, with respect, without judgement and without interruption so that they can clarify their thoughts and express themselves fully.

Best Practice for Active Listening and Reflection

Firstly, be present and pay attention. Give the person speaking your full attention and try to put everything else out of your mind. We have all heard people speak of the wonderful sense of "being the only person in the room" when meeting charismatic politicians, actors, or business leaders. They talk about how the persons full attention was on them and how the person was listening intently to what they said, and they always say how good it made them feel.

This is the skill, the ability to pay full attention and block out the distractions so that you can actually process fully what people are saying. It needs commitment and practice; it is rooted in the ability to be present in a given situation. If you are not able to be present in the moment because of what is going on, then you should rearrange your one to one, catch up or formal coaching session to a time when you can give more focus.

You should also observe body language, facial expressions, and tone of voice as you are listening, to gauge the true meaning behind what is being said. Sometimes the words don't match the tone, facial expression or body language which may be a signal that you should be probing through reflection and open questions.

As you are listening try not to be judgemental or to jump to conclusions, let them finish what they are saying, before you make conclusions. Being judgemental inevitably leads to defensiveness and to the other person closing up or perhaps going on the attack, so hold your judgement and try to listen as a neutral observer.

Mind the Gap! Don't rush to fill the gaps in a conversation if you think the speaker is still processing and thinking. It can be awkward, and it takes a bit of getting used to, but if you think there is more to come then try to wait a few seconds before jumping in.

Active listening is just that, it is an active process designed to help the speaker process their thoughts more clearly and to be able to self-appraise what they are saying. We play an active role by reflecting back what was said through paraphrasing or summarising. It can be a useful way of getting people to reflect back on what they have just said and at the very least you can check that you have understood them correctly. It also serves the purpose of giving the speaker confidence that you are actively listening.

It can be as simple as saying, "So what I understood by what you said is…" or "You said that…"

Questioning

Asking open questions is another way of eliciting information, helping people to think, probing assumptions and drawing insights. Open questions are most useful at the start of a conversation because they get the speaker to think and do not close down alternatives and they avoid you just getting the answer you are looking for.

For example, "Do you like working here?" is a closed question, it will elicit a yes or no answer and does not give much room for an expansive response

Simply changing the question to "What do you think about working here?" or "How do you feel about working here?" is going to get you a different, more expansive answer.

When asking questions, you are trying to find out what the person really thinks and feels. You need to avoid causing defensiveness which tends to get people to close up or go on the attack. "Why" questions can make people defensive. Avoiding why questions is a really simple but effective change you can make that will have a positive impact on the quality of your interactions.

For example, if someone says, "I really think we should reconsider the marketing plan for the new product launch". Asking "Why?" is likely to lead them into a defence of their statement not a further explanation or greater depth.

Whereas you can reframe the question as an open question, such as: "What do think the main issues are?", "What reasons do you have for wanting to reconsider", "Can you give me an example of what we should reconsider?" or simply "Tell me more about that"

All of these questions will lead to further explanation, provide additional useful information and clarification without the speaker feeling the need to defend their position. Use questions to develop clarity of thinking, probe assumptions, discover alternatives, clarify risks and opportunities, gauge confidence and commitment to action.

Example Questions

There is no one set of magic questions as it will depend on the specific situation, however you can think of types of questions being categorised into groups that help you achieve different goals in the conversation. You can use these as a guide to help you have meaningful conversations and to help you coach someone into finding clarity, insight and the action needed to solve their issue.

Clarification
What do you mean by...?
Can you give me an example?
What do you think is the main issue?

Probe Assumptions
What else could we assume?
How did you arrive at these assumptions?
What happens if your assumption is wrong?

Reasoning and Evidence
Can you give me a specific example?
What evidence are you basing your answer on?

Alternatives and choices
> Are there different ways of looking at this problem?
> What other choices do you have?

Focus on Action

To refer back to my definition of coaching, it is goal orientated with a focus on setting objectives and identifying actions that deliver improved performance. And mentoring is helping people to acquire new knowledge, develop new skills and build new behaviours that deliver improved performance.

Coaching and mentoring are not passive activities, they are action focused with the aim of delivering improved performance and achievement of objectives. Throughout the process there should be a focus on creating momentum through actions that help develop the individual or move an objective forward.

The output of any interactions should be clarity on the next steps and clear actions for the coachee to take forward, with milestones and regular review. See Chapter 7 on setting objectives.

Questions you can use to probe action and commitment are:

> How confident are you in achieving the objective?
> On a scale of 1 to 10 how committed are you to this objective?
> What resources do you need?
> When will you achieve the objective?
> What steps do you need to take to achieve the objective

ABC

To paraphrase a famous sales mantra (Always Be Closing),

you should Always Be Coaching. What I mean is that adopting a coaching attitude and approach should become second nature when you are interacting with your team, so that even in informal moments or brief conversations you are using the key techniques we've discussed here.

Listening attentively, using open questions to help them clarify what they mean and think of the possible solutions themselves, before stepping in with the answer for them.

For example, one of your team comes to your desk and says,

"Hey boss, have you got a couple of minutes I need to get your advice on something?"

Your instinct may be to listen to what they have to say (hopefully actively listening) and then to say:

> *"Well, what I think you should do is..." or "Why don't you do X" or even "Oh yeah I know about this, what you need to do is XYZ"*

If we get ourselves into a coaching mindset, we should respond in a different kind of way. For example:

> *"Can you clarify what the main issue is for me?" or "What do you think the next steps should be?", "What would be a good outcome here / what would success look like?", "What options have you thought of?" or simply, "What would you like to do?"*

The specific question will depend on the specific situation and there are many ways of asking, but the point to remember is that we need to get into the habit of supporting our people to think through the possible solutions for themselves, to clarify what they mean, and to be clear on the outcome they are looking for.

Feedback as part of a Coaching Approach

Feedback is an important component of empowering leadership It is necessary to be able to give effective feedback and receive feedback, with a growth mindset.

For most people I think, feedback is both difficult to receive, particularly if given poorly and also difficult to give. It is particularly difficult to give feedback well and for it to be a positive experience for the giver and receiver.

When we hear negative feedback or feedback that challenges our view of ourselves, we have a natural tendency to feel we are under attack or threatened by the feedback. This is particularly true if the negative feedback received goes against a strong view, we have of ourselves or challenges our ego.

When people react badly to feedback, they tend to stop listening and are no longer fully present. The person receiving the feedback, therefore may not really hear or be able to process anything you say after you give the feedback.

There are many organisations that still operate on a tick box annual review model. With tortuous forms to be filled in and annual review meetings. These systems were introduced to ensure that managers sat down with their staff at least once a year to give feedback and talk about objectives for the year. This is setting a minimum benchmark for how a manager should behave and is not a substitute for good leadership. Leaders or managers who use an empowering style, who feedback regularly and have good relationships with their team, do not need the formal annual review. And the leaders who do not regularly feedback need to move to a empowering leadership style, rather than relying on a once a year process of giving out of date, stilted feedback on a person's performance who they haven't spoken to meaningfully all year.

"In a survey of 30,000 employees, only 29% claimed to know if they were doing a good job based on reviews from their bosses. CEB research found that more than 9 in 10 managers are dissatisfied with how their companies conduct annual performance reviews, and almost 9 in 10 HR leaders say current appraisal models don't yield accurate information. When it comes to helping others succeed, traditional feedback hardly draws rave reviews." (Hirsch, 2017).

Feedback should be a regular, ongoing part of a relationship. Feedback should be focused on the things that will make a difference to a person's behaviour and performance, helping deliver change that develops them in their job and helps them grow into future roles. This is where a different way to think about and practice feedback, FeedFoward can be really powerful, and it fits well with a coaching and empowering leadership style.

Feedforward

"Feedforward is a unique approach to giving feedback that improves performance, boosts productivity, and keeps teams on track. Unlike traditional feedback, feedforward is timely, continuous, and focused on development – a refreshing change from the typical feedback fare that rarely makes a positive difference or offers much insight about how work gets done."

(Hirsch, 2017)

This approach differs from the traditional approach to feedback, in that it focuses on future development, rather than getting bogged down in the past, which doesn't help development and growth into the future.

Traditional Negative feedback focuses on shortcomings, and behavioural issues that occurred in the *past*.

Negative Feedforward, however, focuses only on those behaviours may affect future performance, success, or achievements. In other words, the focus is on correcting or neutralising behaviours that may get in the way of your future development and progression. It has a future focused emphasis on the benefits of changing or stopping behaviours, rather than critiquing them. So that the person is motivated by future benefits gained from modifying or stopping their behaviours.

Traditional positive Feedback focuses on past successes or desired behaviour, a "well done" or a "good job"

Positive Feedforward focuses on future benefits of behaviours that will enhance outcomes and results and will help the person achieve their career and performance goals. The person is looking to the future and understands why developing an area of strength or putting more time and effort into something can benefit them or the team in the future.

Instead of focusing on events that can't be changed, the feedback conversation should "link past performance with future work goals, creating a forward-looking feedback narrative meant to encourage employees, not merely critique them." (Hirsch)

The core elements to feedforward are that the feedback given should be timely, continuous, specific, focused on future development and action orientated. There are also some other key elements to giving effective feedback which are the strength of the relationship, where you give feedback, and your body language, tone of voice and facial expressions.

The Relationship

Ideally you should have a good relationship with the person you are giving feedback to, built on mutual respect and with a level of trust. Listen, and ask open questions, the fundamentals of coaching outlined earlier in this chapter, to get an understanding of the person's ego state, opinion of themselves and where they see their strengths and weaknesses. You need to respect them as an individual and ideally, they need to respect you and to know that you have their best interests at heart.

These are key building blocks for a relationship in which feedback has the best chance of been taken in the spirit of learning and growth rather than criticism and threat.

Body language, facial expression, and tone of voice

The mindset that you have should be one of helping the person learn and change rather than one of disappointment, anger, or frustration. Your mindset will drive your behaviour and influence the way you think about how and what you say. Thinking about how you give the feedback is as important as what you say. Being present, self-aware, and making sure you are relaxed when giving feedback will help you achieve the right tone and approach.

The person receiving feedback will have heightened awareness of any signs that you don't mean what you say, or that you are angry or disappointed when giving the feedback. This will cause a defensive reaction and will not help you land your feedback nor help the receiver grow and develop.

Try to control your body language, expressions, and tone of voice to give feedback in a neutral or positive way so that it is your words that carry the weight and meaning. The receiver then has a better chance of taking the feedback neutrally or positively.

Place and Time

Where and when you give feedback is another vital element. We have all witnessed, experienced, or committed the cardinal sin of attempting to give feedback when the situation or time are not appropriate. Some examples are in front of other people (when not in a group feedback session), immediately after the event in question when emotions are running high. It could be in a busy and noisy environment where things can be misconstrued, or when negative feedback is left until the end of a meeting so that the consequences of any negative reactions do not have to be endured and an escape can be made.

Feedback should be given at the appropriate time, in the appropriate setting. In terms of timing, this should not be immediately after the event or witnessed behaviour, unless it is a quick "well done", any more detailed feedback needs to be done after a small gap in time. But just as importantly it should not be left for too long. This reduces the ability to accurately recall and reduces the impact because it is less vivid in the mind of the receiver.

Ideally you are looking at feedback being given regularly and close in time to the events or behaviour in question. I would want to have both positive and negative feedback given within a few days ideally, and no more than 7 days out from the event in question. That way it is fresh in people's minds and the recall is easier for both parties. How things "felt" can also still be accessed, which is important.

Feedback early feels relevant and important and not an afterthought or tick box exercise in a scheduled annual or half yearly review. If it's worth giving feedback on, it's worth doing regularly throughout the year as things happen.

In terms of where you should give the feedback it is partly dependent on your relationship and the nature of the feedback, but always make sure it is sufficiently private, quiet, and away from the desk and daily work.

If it is serious negative feedback that is touching on a potentially difficult area, then this should be more formal and structured, and you should leave plenty of time. Other feedback can be given over coffee or in a short meeting but as long as you focus on feedback and learning.

Specific and relevant areas for development

Feedback should be focused on what is most helpful to the person receiving it, based on their goals, objectives and needs at the time. You should focus in on the details and behaviours that matter and not worry about feedback on those that don't. Feedback should be about things that are critical to job performance or future development potential.

Remember to think about what is going to be useful for the receiver to help motivate them, achieve their goals, and improve performance. Keeping feedback specific, focused, and regular makes it easier to give richer more relevant feedback and makes it more actionable.

Actionable Feedback

By keeping feedback specific and forward looking it becomes easier to also make the feedback actionable. It must be something that the receiver can do something with. Broad based generic comments or platitudes are not helpful because the receiver can't action a change.

You should be aiming not to overwhelm people with lots of areas of change or with big steps, rather think about how to break down feedback into actionable chunks that are uncomplicated steps on the road to improvement and that can be demonstrated, measured, and reviewed.

If we are trying to work on a behavioural change to improve someone's collaboration with others, we need to break this down into less daunting and more actionable feedback objectives. For example, "You need to be more collaborative" is generic and hard to do anything about.

But by building a plan of actions that will lead to greater collaboration we can break this down into less daunting achievable objectives that the person can accomplish and in doing so they will become more collaborative. For example, the first three objectives to be worked on one at a time, could be:

1.   Bring one issue or question to each team meeting and ask for input
2.   Join a project team that needs your specific skills to help resolve an issue
3.   Before putting your next project plan into action make a list of all the people who it affects or who may have valuable knowledge and consult with them about the project.

Think of behavioural objectives in the same way as task or process objectives, despite them feeling more difficult to define to begin with. By breaking down behavioural development objectives into bite size objectives that are easy to understand, action orientated, and measurable, people become much more motivated to make changes and develop their behavioural skills one step at a time.

Your Objectives and Actions from this Chapter

- Adopt the behaviours of a coaching mentor
- Build meaningful relationships with your team members
- Understand the capacity and capability of your team members
- Always Be Coaching
- Listen actively, reflect back, and ask open questions
- Practice Feedfoward – regularly, timely and in an appropriate location
- Think about body language, tone of voice and facial expressions – aiming for neutral or positive
- Make feedback specific and focused only on things that will benefit the receiver and improve performance
- Coaching and Feedback should be focused on action through agreeing well-defined objectives

9. Principle 6 – Emotional Safety

"It is fine to celebrate success, but it is more important to heed the lessons from failure."

Bill Gates

Emotional safety (or psychological safety) is: "A shared belief held by members of a team that the team is safe for interpersonal risk taking" (Amy Edmundson, 2018).

As we discussed in Chapter 2, psychological or emotional safety is a critical component of the culture of high performing teams. This is because high levels of emotional safety make it possible for people to learn together without the fear of being ridiculed, ignored, or blamed.

Being able to share your thoughts, knowing that you have a voice in the team and being confident that you can share learnings from both successes and failures boosts confidence, mutual learning, and creative thinking.

To build a culture of emotional safety within your team you need to establish team norms that support it. The two key components that have been found in high performance teams demonstrating high levels of emotional safety are:

- Firstly, they have high instances of "conversational turn-taking" i.e., everyone has a voice. All members of the team are respected and encouraged to share their thoughts, and they are listened to actively by the group.
- Secondly, they have high levels of "average social

sensitivity'', or empathy within the group. Most people are aware of the importance of empathy in developing emotional intelligence.

This was supported by a study conducted by a group of psychologists from Carnegie Mellon, M.I.T. and Union College (2010) that found: "...converging evidence of a general collective intelligence factor that explains a group's performance on a wide variety of tasks. This "c factor" is not strongly correlated with the average or maximum individual intelligence of group members but is correlated with the average social sensitivity of group members, the equality in distribution of conversational turn-taking..."

As was found in the Google Aristotle research these high performing teams were, "free from fear and ego, where people can speak up, make mistakes, question things, and raise concerns without humiliation or retribution." (NYT, 2016) And in a study published in the Journal of Organizational Behaviour, "Researchers are finding that psychological safety may be the No. 1 aspect of successful teams, driving creativity and innovation." (Hood et el, 2016)

Building a culture where people feel psychologically or emotionally safe to speak up and be honest boosts motivation, engagement, and performance. It creates a culture where learning can happen, and creativity and innovation can thrive. It also plays a role in delivering inclusivity in the workplace, by definition if you have high levels of emotional safety you are going to have high levels of inclusivity.

In conclusion there is a high correlation between high

performance and how a team treat one another.

Creating a culture of emotional safety where views, opinions, and mistakes can be shared openly in a safe environment, means that the team can learn together and capitalise on the collective intelligence of the group to deliver better performance, consistently over time.

Developing an Emotionally Safe Culture

Whilst many people will naturally gravitate to some of the key behaviours that make up an emotionally safe culture, many will find it more difficult, and most will not land on all of the elements without a conscious effort to do so.

There are things you can do that will help foster the right environment and give people the tools to operate in a way that's supports a positive learning culture.

Role Modelling

Establishing an emotionally safe environment is not possible if the leader of the team does not model the correct behaviour. Leaders need to act as role models, modelling the behaviour necessary and setting the tone for the rest of the team to follow. A leader's influence on the culture and atmosphere under which the team operates is so powerful that it can completely overpower the rest of the team in a negative way, or it can have a very positive impact on encouraging desirable behaviour.

As a leader you need to display the key characteristics and behaviours that will signal to your team that they are in an emotionally safe environment. Your behaviour rather than your merely your words will be what lets people know what you really think.

You should establish an environment in which team members can challenge behaviour that is not acceptable or conducive to a learning environment by demonstrating the right behaviours consistently. There is nothing more likely to shatter believe and trust than the boss being hypocritical or acting from the position of "do as I say, not do as I do."

Every person is different, and some will need more time and encouragement than others to trust you and the culture they are in, so you need to understand that it may take a bit of time to establish a truly open environment where everyone feels good about opening up.

We have talked about a lot of the behaviours required by leaders to engender emotional safety in the previous chapters, the principal ones being:

- High levels of self-awareness and the ability to manage their emotional state
- Take a personal interest in others
- Low personal ego - successful when their team is successful
- Learn through two-way feedback
- Employ empathy, actively listen, and treat people with respect
- Use coaching and mentoring to develop and guide
- A growth and learning mindset

In modelling the behaviour needed for high levels of emotional safety you, as a leader, firstly need to be in control of your emotions and your behaviour. Try to control your body language, expressions, and tone of voice when responding or talking to the team. Use a neutral or positive tone so that it is your words that carry the weight and meaning and not the way you come across. Being present, self-aware, and making sure you are relaxed when listening will help you achieve this approach.

It takes a little bit of time for people to work their way to being more open and honest but if your reaction and responses are supportive, they will open up and become more emboldened. You will then be able to get honest input into decision making, valuable feedback and hear about learnings from mistakes and failures, as well as successes.

You can make your job easier by establishing a team charter with the group, that sets down agreed behavioural norms and standards expected by all, and importantly what is not acceptable. More on this later in this chapter.

Taking a genuine interest in others, using the skills of active listening, reflection, and open questions (that were covered in detail in Chapter 8) will help you model the right behaviour for emotional safety to thrive. When people feel they are being genuinely listened to and that the person they are speaking to is taking a real interest then they are more likely to trust the person. They will feel like they have a voice and that their opinion matters, even if in the end an alternative route is chosen. People are less likely to feel aggrieved about decisions going against their position if they have had a fair chance to put their views across and have been taken seriously. When they feel they were heard along with others and a final decision has been taken in the full knowledge of everyone's views it is much easier to get people on board and take collective responsibility as a team.

Openness and Situational Leadership

Another behaviour to model is that of openness. A willingness to admit mistakes, and acknowledge what you don't know, deferring to others where your knowledge is lacking.

The ability to do this is closely linked to the level self-esteem, mindset, and ego a leader has. High levels of self-esteem, a growth mindset and low levels of ego will mean you are more willing and able to be open to learning with your team and enabling situational leadership when relevant and beneficial.

My definition of situational leadership as used here, is the willingness to pass over leadership of a meeting or project in which you are involved to a member of your team, with you playing an active role as a team member. I would often say in a meeting that I want someone else to lead this meeting based on expertise, knowledge or ownership of the project or business area in hand. I would simply say at the start of the meeting "Mary is leading this meeting today, I'm here as part of the team." This way the rest of the group know your position in the meeting and that "Mary" is the owner of this project has the leadership role. If you have delegated authority and ownership, then it makes no sense to step in to lead a meeting when you happen to be involved just because you are the leader, be comfortable playing the part of a team member.

Everybody has a Voice

At the start of this chapter, I reasserted the research on the power of high levels of emotional safety to drive learning and in turn high performance through continual improvement, creativity, and innovation.

One of the key elements of the research was the prevalence of conversational turn taking in high performing teams, in other words everyone has a voice. This is clearly something the whole team has to buy in to and they have to learn how to help facilitate this important facet. But once again as a leader you can model this behaviour, as you are in the perfect position to do so.

You can make sure that people are listened to and if they are interrupted you can politely interject and ask that they be allowed to finish.

Conversely if someone is hogging the conversation you can politely ask them to yield by thanking them for their contribution, stating that we need to move on to someone else in the interests of time and to enable more people to have their say.

If there are members of the team who haven't volunteered to speak then you can ask them if they would like to add anything. Or simply say that you would really like to hear what they think. Remember if you build an emotionally safe culture even the most reticent and introverted members should feel safe to speak up.

You can take this a step further and use a technique that Nancy Kline (author of "Time to Think") recommends where you formally establish a meeting etiquette that gives everyone a chance to speak in turn, and to be listened to actively. You explain this process at the beginning of the meeting and go around the room one by one, having instructed the group that they need to actively listen and not interrupt, make notes of questions, and allow the speaker time to think.

Remember listening actively, non-judgementally and without interruption will elicit the best thinking from everyone. As Nancy Kline so elegantly puts it, "The quality of your attention determines the quality of other people's thinking" (1999).

Inclusivity

Before I talk about establishing a team charter, I want to talk a little bit about inclusivity and the importance of being conscious of promoting and maintaining an inclusive atmosphere that is enabled by the culture you have created.

The definition of inclusivity is closely aligned to the definition of emotional safety, the CIPD define it in the following way, "Workplace inclusion is when people feel valued and accepted in their team and in the wider organisation, without having to conform." In other words, they feel emotionally safe to be themselves and this should be accompanied by the feeling that they are not going to be offended or be made to feel they are outside of the group in anyway. This is where a team charter can work well, as it gives everyone a chance to input and to make sure the way people behave reflects their feelings and sensibilities.

When people are relaxed with each other and confident enough to joke and have fun, and sometimes at others expense it can feel like a great culture. I have been in teams like this and as a sales director I am very familiar with this kind of "knockabout" culture, where there are a lot of extrovert and confident people. The thing

I learned that even in teams when most of the banter is accepted, most of the time, and there is no malicious intent, it only takes one or two occasions for the joke to go too far or for some people to find it intimidating, offensive or both. So, banter, ribbing, joking and sarcasm, may be the sign of a good culture as far as the people in the team are concerned, but as teams become larger and / or more diverse it may well offend some and can at worst become toxic.

Respecting each and every team member is only possible if you are cognisant of the fact that everyone will have different sensibilities, sensitivities, and tolerances. Once a team becomes diverse and / or a certain size (beyond 5 or 6) you cannot assume that the team is homogeneous and that everyone shares the same level of confidence, sense of humour, and personality disposition.

I am not advocating a humourless team culture, that would be very poor in many other ways. Levity and fun are important ingredients in an effective team, but whilst appropriate humour is a good thing, sarcasm, ribbing about personality traits or jokes at the expense of others (even if the person being joked about is ok with it) are not ok in a team environment where there is wide diversity of people and backgrounds, or a large group, as there are too many possibilities for it to go wrong.

When assessing the culture of a large team I was working with, that was fairly diverse, with a good level of emotional safety, it became clear that as new people joined the leadership failed to take seriously enough the impact on team culture of the resulting increase in diversity (in terms of age, sexual orientation, personality type and ethnicity). They had also not realised the difficulty for some new starters of joining a well-established culture with its own norms of behaviour. Even if it was generally considered a well meaning positive culture. There was a genuine desire to create an inclusive culture with high levels of emotional safety but they lacked a complete understanding of what was required.

The increase in diversity was a positive thing that led to a more creative and dynamic team, but it also meant that some of the new joiners felt that they did not fit into the culture and also that some of the accepted banter was inappropriate and offended their sensibilities.

Additionally, when this was raised with the leadership, they discovered that some existing members of the team were not as comfortable as others with the tone of some elements of the culture but had not said anything. This was particularly true of the younger members of the team who had joined in the last two years.

Despite the leadership making a great job of building a high performing team, the level of emotional safety was not high enough and the diversity in the team was not catered for effectively enough, in other words there was diversity without true inclusivity.

This was an eye opening and sobering moment for the leader, it was shock to realise the culture was failing some people and was not as inclusive as had been assumed.

There are number of lessons from this example to do with team dynamics and culture.

Firstly, you cannot assume that culture is static; it will continually evolve. You need to take regular soundings and make sure to seek out opinions of wide spectrum of people.

Secondly you need to recognise diversity in all its forms and move from merely championing diversity to engendering true inclusivity, by ensuring that you understand the sensibilities of everyone in the team by getting to know them, or when running a large team ensuring your immediate reports know their people well.

Finally, as new members join the team it is important to be able to explain the culture, values, and team norms clearly and allow them to respond to them in an open way with their thoughts and feelings. A team charter helps to do this also and it should be updated when the make-up of the team changes if there are things that it does not adequately capture.

Lost in translation...another common element of modern teams is the diversity of nationalities, with the difference in cultural touch points and language understanding, which can lead easily to misunderstandings.

For example, working with a finance director in Asia who is part of an international management meeting, he became concerned about a comment made during one of these meetings. His boss's boss made a joke about him. He said that he "was sleeping at work because he did not have enough work to do due to sales being slow."

The person making the joke was a native speaker and it later transpired meant nothing negative by the comment with regard to the finance director it was aimed it at. It was in fact a dig at the sales function for not providing finance with enough work to do due to poor sales.

However, the finance director (who speaks English as a second language and was from a very different culture) did not understand the joke or what it was referring to and understood it as the regional boss being critical. The worry caused by this misunderstanding lasted for several weeks, until it was explained.

The culture you are building needs to work for everyone and everyone needs to feel safe to be themselves, have their say and try new things. This can only be achieved if all elements of the way the team interacts with each other have been considered.

You will not get it right all the time and mistakes are bound to be made, but the important thing is to approach with the right mindset and the best of intentions.

Team Charter

All members have a role to play in ensuring that the team operates a culture that supports challenge, learning and creativity. As a leader you can model the behaviours and set the tone through your behaviour, but clearly the team need to buy into it, and they need to exhibit the right behaviours as well.

Consistent with the rest of this book the norms and agreed behaviours accepted by the team need to be shared, so they need to be debated and decided upon as a team.

Creating a team charter or contract together that defines the norms for team behaviour enables the team to align on what's expected of each other and what's not expected or is unacceptable.

Use an open brainstorming and open session, facilitated by someone external to your team, either internally or an external coach, to help ensure everyone is heard and all opinions are captured. And use a format that suits the team culture to capture and display your agreed charter.

The charter should capture all opinions and be a useful reference document that can be publicised and shared with all team members and new team members as they join.

New team members can be encouraged to give their views and share any suggested amendments. It enables you to check for inclusivity and evolve your charter as the team evolves avoiding the culture becoming cliquey or too inwardly focused.

You should review it annually anyway and more often when you first start using it. For the first 3 months or so you should be checking back to see if it is doing its job and taking feedback and suggestions on board as a team.

It might look something like this:

Example Team Charter

We agree as a team to abide by the following principles in the spirit of creating an emotionally safe, challenging, creative learning environment that involves all team members and fosters continual improvement, innovation, and high performance.

IN	OUT
Listening to each other— we all get a turn	Playing politics
Being open to ideas	Passive aggressive comments
Supporting each other	Not airing thoughts
Sharing our mistakes and fails	Being negative about others
Learning together	Rushing to blame
Challenge with Respect	Not being collaborative
Bad News Early!	Group think
Be Present and Be Prepared	Putting internal politics before the customer
No Meeting Wednesdays	Meetings for meetings sake
Assume positive motivation behind behaviours	Talking over and interrupting in meetings
Seek to understand first	
Focus on, and Fight for the customer/consumer	

Clearly this is not an exhaustive list, nor does it suit every type of team, but it provides an example of the kind of things that can be agreed upon, to be included and excluded.

Imagine how much easier and less confrontational it is for all team members, even the most junior to challenge someone else's behaviour when they can simply refer to a charter they have signed up to. Instead of calling someone out based on what the other person thinks of their behaviour you can point to the charter, just by saying, "hey, that's not how we all agreed we would behave in the charter."

The Charter for Project Driven Environments

Team charters can also be really useful for project teams.

Project based teams and collaborative cross functional working are becoming the norm in many businesses. And in some industries, such as Software development project teams are the norm. One study, found that "the time spent by managers and employees in collaborative activities has ballooned by 50 percent or more over the last two decades" (HBR 2016) and in many companies, more than three-quarters of an employee's day is spent communicating with colleagues.

One significant challenge for any project team is forming and establishing norms of behaviour quickly and effectively given the temporary and diverse nature of the teams, some, or many, of whom may not have worked together.

Spending half a day in workshop at the beginning of the project to agree a team charter using a sensible templated charter that includes the fundamentals of good teamwork as a start point, can really help the process. The workshop itself is good for the team members to get to know each other and it gives an opportunity to work out up front how the team wants to operate. Of course, many companies have established contracts or charters that they use for project teams (many don't) but they are often imposed templates with no chance for discussion, addition, or amendment. This does not create a shared sense of ownership and buy-in to the team charter that a workshop does.

Challenge

One of the benefits of creating a positive, open, no blame culture using the model and principles contained in this book, is that you and your team can challenge more. Great ideas come from a culture of debate and challenge. If people feel confident and able to speak their mind and share their thoughts, they are more willing to challenge each other in a constructive way to build on ideas and reach the best decisions. And if you have agreed the "rules of engagement" in your team charter it gives people a framework in which to challenge and share alternative viewpoints.

A learning culture will mean a less defensive culture and a less defensive culture is a better environment for sharing opinions, challenging ideas, and presenting alternatives. This is because you have created an environment where there is a framework to challenge and a support structure so people can stretch themselves and try new things.

As discussed in Chapter 6 discussion, challenge and presenting alternatives leads to better decision making, which in turn leads to a more successful high performing team.

Disruptive and Underperforming Team Members

You may be wondering why this topic appears in the chapter on emotional safety. Having the right people in your team who can consistently display the right behaviours to create a high performing team is critical. The two aspects that are going to get the right people in your team are recruitment and how you are able to develop and coach the team you have. Sometimes as you well know, there are those who do not fit with the team, either because they are underperforming in their key tasks or against their objectives or because their attitude and behaviours do not fit with the agreed culture of the team.

We can either coach and develop people to improve their performance against behavioural or task objectives so that they become a valuable member of the team, or we may have to exit them because they are unable to improve their performance, or they are having a negative effect on the team and are not conducive to its success.

We have covered a lot of aspects of building, developing and nurturing talent in the previous chapters on coaching, feedback, and leadership approach. Here I want to cover having difficult conversations, which the vast majority of people find hard. How a company chooses to manage the review or exit of an employee will be down to their HR policies, this is not the place for an in-depth discussion these policies, but what I want to help with is having those difficult conversations.

Difficult conversations are defined as the conversations that go beyond the coaching and feedback techniques covered in Chapter 8, with people who are being disruptive, refusing to fit in with agreed norms of behaviour or underperforming against key objectives and are not responding well to coaching and feedback.

Difficult Conversations

Dealing successfully with situations that are emotionally charged and that have serious consequences for the ego and self-image of a person and/or their career and livelihood is tough for anyone who has a normal level of emotional intelligence and empathy. This means we often find it difficult to react in a calm and unemotional way, and the true reasonable meaning of what we want to say can get lost. This can lead to defensive, negative, or aggressive reactions from the other person and resolution or getting the outcome we want is difficult to achieve.

As a leader you are going to have to have more of these conversations than most people. There is a method you can use to handle these situations and to dramatically improve the outcomes you obtain, as well as increasing the emotional safety for both parties in the conversation. Being truly assertive using neutral language, is highly effective for managing difficult and sensitive conversations, and for dealing with conflict.

Assertive Communication

True assertiveness is not in any way aggressive or pushy and it's not about making demands. In fact, assertiveness is the opposite of aggressive. It is about controlling and modulating how we communicate, our body language, the words we speak and the tone we use.

Assertiveness at its heart is about taking the judgement and negative emotions out what is said. It is about understanding and empathising with the other persons point of view to neutralise the language, body language and tone and in turn reduce the possible negative emotional response. Assertive communication allows you to express positive and negative ideas and feelings in an open, honest, and direct way. To assert your point of view and needs, whilst still being considerate to the other person.

Assertive communication can help make you a better leader, because you will be clear, honest, empathetic, and fair minded in your communication when you need to have a more difficult conversation. You treat people with respect and people know where they stand with you and what you expect. It's also an important part of negotiating with and influencing customers and internal stakeholders.

The first step in having a successful outcome from a difficult conversation is setting your-self up for success .

- Self-awareness, think about how you express what you feel,

need, believe, or want
- Prepare in advance, if possible, think about what and how you are going to say something, and also ensuring you get to say what you need to say
- Manage the meeting and control the agenda. Be persistent and don't be put off by the reaction of the other person or allow them to divert the conversation to another topic. Ensure you say what you intended to say
- Remember you are not responsible for how the other person reacts to your assertiveness the only thing you can control is how well you put your point of view across
- Repeat yourself, if need be, to ensure the message is properly heard, always remaining calm and clear in what you want.

As with giving feedback (Chapter 8) when you have the conversation is also important. It is better to have the conversation as close to the observed behaviour or underperformance happening as possible. This means the observations are more likely to be accurate and it makes it more difficult for the person to deny recollection or push back on the veracity of what you are saying.

Using Non-Violent Communication

A good place to start to help understand and build a model for assertive communication is Nonviolent Communication developed by Michael B. Rosenberg (Nonviolent communication: a language of compassion, 1999).

As Rosenberg states: "When we express our needs indirectly

through the use of evaluations, interpretations, and images, others are likely to hear criticism. And when people hear anything that sounds like criticism, they tend to invest their energy in self-defence or counterattack" (Rosenberg 2015)

Using Rosenberg's work, we can call on a framework of steps that help us develop an assertive non-violent communication style using four simple steps.

1. Observe and assess the situation

The first step is to listen actively and observe effectively and withhold judgment. Listening attentively enables us to better understand what the other person is saying, it's only through understanding others can we empathise effectively with others (see Chapter 8 for more on active listening). To help express your observations without judgement, you need to be as specific and factual as possible. Using specific examples of observed behaviour rather than an opinion or hearsay.

2. Express how you feel

Express your feelings in a clear and open way to enable the other person to know what affect their behaviour is having on the team, the company or you. Many of us are not used to expressing feelings specifically and will need to think about what we are going to say. As in the first step it is important to be specific to help the listener understand what's going on inside rather than using vague statements.

3. Communicate your needs

It is important to communicate what you would like to happen or what you need the other person to do in clear unambiguous terms. This helps the other person to understand what they can do about their behaviour. They may not agree with everything, or they may not be able to give you what you want, but they will at least know what the need is and be able to address it directly. Once again, we need to be specific. Often in difficult situations we may be vague in expressing what we need from the other person, this leads to a situation where neither side is satisfied because you have not really expressed your needs and the other person has not been given a fair crack to do something about it.

4. Express what you would like to happen

Finally, we make a specific request to change something or express the need for something to happen. Using the phrase "would you please" or "could you please". The request needs to be as clear and specific as possible and presented in positive language. Positive language means asking for something to be done or action to be taken to start, modify or stop something.

Here are a couple of examples using NVC in situations you may face in a work environment:

"You are always missing deadlines. It is frustrating and annoying when you miss deadlines, it causes me problems with my deadlines. You have to make sure you hit deadlines from now on."

This is quite a common way of expressing frustration to an underperforming employee. Think about this short statement and you can see it is loaded with emotion, it is non-specific and likely an exaggeration borne of frustration. It is likely to illicit a defensive reaction.

Using NVC we would rephrase this statement to make it specific and focused on individual occurrences that you can point to, which is less likely to provoke a defensive reaction. We would also include a specific expression of how it makes you feel and what you would like the other person to do about it.

It would be more like this:

"You have missed agreed deadlines on three occasions in the last month. This makes me feel like you are not understanding the importance of deadlines. Hitting deadlines is a key performance measure for your role and missing deadlines has a knock-on effect on others in the team. So you need to be able to meet deadlines to perform in your role. I would like you to consider what is causing you to miss deadlines and talk to me about what you will do differently and what support you may need, to ensure you hit deadlines going forward."

This is firstly not expressing any anger and secondly it is much clearer for the listener what the issue is. It is neutral and straightforward and specific to the situation in hand. It is difficult to react defensively because the speaker is expressing how something makes them feel. This statement tells them precisely what your need is, why it is important and what you want them to do about.

Let's look at another example of managing a difficult conversation with a difficult team member. Let's use the example situation of a team member who is disruptive because they don't listen to others and talk over people. This behaviour is damaging team moral and is not good for the emotional safety in the team.

Many people would handle this by saying something like:

"Your behaviour is creating a bad atmosphere in the team; you are being aggressive and rude. I and others have noticed it and it's not how you should be behaving towards others. You should not be behaving in this way and it's not good for the atmosphere in the team."

You can imagine a defensive reaction to this, it's vague and it does not address what you want the person to do differently to fix the situation.

Using NVC it would sound something like this:

"In yesterday's meeting I witnessed you interrupt Sue and be dismissive to Bob when they were talking. This makes me feel that you are not considering others needs and the team members in question have told me it makes them feel frustrated that they are not being listened to and their ideas are being shot down. Listening to and respecting other people's opinions is an important part of your role and of

being a member of this team, so I need this behaviour to stop. Could you please take time to consider your behaviour and then talk to me about why you are behaving in this way and what you could do differently to resolve this."

In this example you are talking about specific observed behaviour that has happened in the recent past. Secondly you are expressing how you and the other team members feel about the behaviour. Then you are clearly expressing what you need to happen to fix the situation and why. Finally, you are putting the responsibility on them to reflect on their behaviour, explain it and on how to fix it. The emphasis is on them, as with coaching (Chapter 8) to think about their own behaviour and take ownership for changing it.

Your Objectives and Actions from this Chapter

- Work on your own self-awareness and openness
- Practice and model the behaviours that will enable an emotionally safe learning culture
- Encourage and coach the team on the appropriate behaviours
- Establish a Team Charter
- Ensure everyone has a voice
- Focus on creating inclusivity from diversity
- Support situational leadership
- Encourage challenge and alternative views in the team
- Practice Assertive Communication and NVC

10. Principle 7 – Provide, Protect and Champion

'Great things in business are never done
by one person. They're done by
a team of people.'

Steve Jobs

As covered in the opening chapters of this book there are still some managers and leaders who are first and foremost focused on their own power, position, and success. They are led by personal ego and a drive to win and protect their own position above their team or people they employ. They believe in more of a control centred leadership model and the need for personal success drives their decision making and communication style. In short, they do not put people or their team first.

Some organisations still support and perpetuate this approach by rewarding individual performance and putting a premium on individual delivery over that of the team. As this book has hopefully demonstrated this focus on individual performance is not fit for purpose for the modern organisation and is at odds with the type of leadership necessary to create high performing teams, which in turn create high performing organisations capable of delivering sustainable results.

What is required instead is a people first focus by leaders, with the emphasis on their team. To do this they need to change their mindset from one of viewing their team as a means for their personal glory to a mindset where they see themselves as part of the team and their success inextricably linked to the team.

A survey of leaders found that whilst there is still be a need for leaders of dynamic organisations to have a clear vision and be able to articulate that to the business they will, "...need to understand that they don't have to have all the answers – but do need to ask the right questions and have a team surrounding them who are just as passionate about the vision as they are," (Grant Thornton Global, 2022)

There is also an ethical dimension to putting people and your team first. This quote on leadership ethics from Dr S. Ciulla highlights the important role leaders have in using their position to protect and lead ethically. "Leadership is a relationship between the leader and the followers. Ethics is about human relations...the greatest ethical challenge comes from the temptation of power itself. For with leaders' abilities to abuse their power, there comes the power to cover up their misdeeds." (Ciulla 2003, p.323).

If as a leader you are focused on your own success rather than seeing your success as inextricably linked to your team, you are more at risk of abusing the relationship between you and your team. By focusing on your own success, you are by definition going to protect your position and success first and foremost. By following the model proposed in this book you will be working in an ethical way as a leader, because everything you do is based on improving the capacity, capability, and performance of your team. You will be putting your team first because you believe your success is based on the team's success.

With this final principle I am focusing on the importance of securing the resources for your team to perform at its best, secondly to protect your team from external interference, pressure, or unnecessary stress and thirdly to act as a champion and advocate for your team. All of this is made easier if you get out of the way and empower your team because it frees up some of your time to spend on the things that can help your team perform at its best.

Securing Resources

A leader should work to secure the resources required by their team to be successful through network influence, the use of data, and insight. No one will argue with the fact that we can only be successful if we have sufficient resources for the job in hand. I am referring to resources here in the broadest sense, including money, people, training, coaching, systems, processes, and time. Building your network influence as a collaborator and the reputation of your people as a team that works well with others and delivers results will help secure stakeholder support and resources.

You should be very clear when asking for the resources you and your team need to succeed. Demonstrate what can be achieved with the resource you need. Equally you can be forthright about the consequences of not getting the resources you need, in terms of risks to timings, quality, cost or overall delivery. Use data, insight, and information and make your arguments simple and clear, showing that it's in the company's best interests to provide what your team needs.

At the same time, you need to retain a collaborative approach that is focused on what's best for the organisation, as delivered through your team. Avoid becoming parochial about your team and be careful not to become confrontational or negative about other teams to get what you need. Remain a team player, make it clear that your strategic goals are aligned to those of the business and that resourcing your team will benefit the organisation and the other teams you collaborate with.

Lead a high performing team! By following the model in this book to become a leader that delivers a safe, positive, forward-looking culture that delivers innovative solutions you will put you and your team in a strong position to receive the resources you need. Successful teams that are collaborative and add value to the organisation, led by a leader with a strong network are more likely to be well supported.

Know how the organisation works, understand where the blockages are, who has the influence and how to make it work in your favour. Network and influence your way through the organisation so that you can unblock barriers, and work around unnecessary bureaucracy. A big part of your role as a leader is to spend a significant amount of time both internally and externally building mutually beneficial relationships, understanding how things work and how to get the most out of the people the processes and the systems. Building a self-managed learning team based on the model espoused here will allow you to get out of the way to free up your time to dedicate this pursuit.

Act as Filter and a Dam

The old adage is that the pressure flows downhill, and I am sure we have all worked in businesses or for bosses where this is the case. In the worst cases the pressure is simply passed straight down the line to the lowest level of the organisation because if the leader at the top simply passes on the pressure to their direct reports, you can bet the direct reports will usually follow the example set.

If you want your team to be successful you need act as a filter and sometimes a dam. The best leaders do not simply pass the pressure down the line or take out their stress on their team, they learn to manage the stress within themselves and focus on motivating and encouraging their team, keeping unnecessary stress to a minimum. This does not mean sheltering them from reality, expectations, or performance goals but it does mean ensuring that the message is given in an appropriate and motivational way and that there is support for them in achieving their goals. In other words, work out what your team need to know and communicate it in an engaging way.

People and teams perform best with goals that stretch them and there should be high expectations on behaviour and performance with the objective for continual improvement. If, within this context, you want them to perform at their best, you should shield them from any additional stresses, criticism or influences that are not helpful in achieving the teams' goals. In the same way the best sports coaches and managers do when protecting their players so they can concentrate on the game. As Robert I. Sutton notes in his article for the Harvard Business Review, "The best bosses...take pride in being human shields, absorbing or deflecting heat from inside and outside the company..." (Sutton, HBR.org, 2010)

Protecting the team from unnecessary and unhelpful pressure, criticism and other stressors not only helps protect mental and physical well-being it also improves productivity. We are all aware of the negative impact of too much stress and anxiety on our performance and our health. A 2021 review of research across several disciplines highlighted some of the key impacts of stress on workplace productivity.

"Stress negatively affects relationships with co-workers and leads to being mentally checked out at work" and makes it more difficult for people to focus, make decisions and prioritise, which negatively impacts productivity. They also found, "As stress mounts, people disengage from their work and their companies. A Gallup study found "lack of engagement at work costs the U.S. economy $450 billion to $550 billion each year." Conversely when people are happier their productivity increases. A study at call centres in the U.K. found a causal link between happiness and productivity, measuring a 13 percent increase in productivity. (stress.org)

Even the most selfish and controlling leader would struggle to argue that a team that is feeling chronic stress and anxiety is going to perform at their best, even before we consider their mental and physical well-being. Yes, high performing teams work at their best under pressure to perform, but only if the context of that pressure is within a culture of support and emotional safety. People understand the need to hit targets and deadlines, the need to change, innovate and compete, but this is pressure enough, there is no need for additional stress, criticism, or unrealistic demands that will simply damage productivity.

Managing Change

Managing change is a constant for managers, and effective leadership as described in this book includes a focus on continual improvement, development of the team and the way the team operates. In addition to the team dynamics there will be organisational change programs to manage and implement, as well as changes brought on by technology, the market, and the competition. The pace of change and level of task complexity is high in today's organisations, and your job as a leader includes helping to navigate, prioritise and manage the amount of change your team is confronted with, as well as how it is implemented.

By following the model outlined in the previous chapters of this book, you will be able to manage change much more effectively. When implemented all of the principles, behaviours and techniques outlined in this book, help to build an environment and culture where managing change becomes an integral part of the way the team works. A positive learning culture with high levels of emotional safety, effective delegation, two-way feedback and a good understanding of the teams' capabilities and capacity help create an environment where change can be effectively managed.

A word on specifically helping to protect the team in the context of change initiatives. As discussed in more detail in Chapter 7 people's capacity for change and taking on new challenges is not infinite. It is important to take account of both people's capabilities and their capacity when introducing change initiatives.

Capacity refers to an individual's ability to absorb change or take on new tasks effectively. People can only take on a certain amount of new knowledge, tasks or change before they become overloaded, the consequences of which may include, underperformance, burnout, depression, or anxiety.

Capability refers to the skills and knowledge required for a particular task. A person may have the capacity to change, but lack certain key capabilities, which you can build to ensure they have the ability and confidence to take on the task.

Understanding the capacity for change and the capabilities of the team and individuals within it will help you manage the way change is implemented more successfully. To help protect your team and enable them to perform at their best whilst incorporating change you need to choose workplace change initiatives consciously and prioritise them, balancing the needs of the business with workload balance, stress, and capability. Providing the necessary support to build capability and help boost capacity.

Communication and listening to feedback are once again critical factors in managing change by ensuring that people understand the why behind the change, that they have an honest view of the impact on them and their job and that they are given a chance to be heard and to feedback on the proposals.

Communicate early and honestly and make time to listen to feedback and ideas about the change and its implementation. When people feel they are being genuinely listened to then they feel that their opinion matters, even if in the end they cannot fundamentally change the proposal. People are likely to feel more positive about accepting a change if they have had a fair chance to put their views across, have been taken seriously and that the final decision has been taken in the full knowledge of everyone's views.

Getting a level of buy in and acceptance, even if it is not joyful excitement about a process or technological change, makes it easier to implement. The process of talking to people will also enable you to get feedback on how the change will impact people and their roles and you will learn a lot about how best to implement it and what other priorities you need to work around.

Protect them from Time Killers

Meetings are one of the biggest time killers in any organisation. The three problems with meetings are firstly, there are often too many of them. Secondly, they are often too long, and thirdly they are often badly managed.

You can play your part in controlling your own use of meetings with your team. As a leader one of my objectives was to have my team in meetings with me for as little time as possible. In fact, my aversion to meetings was perhaps a little too strong and being self-aware I sat down with my leadership team, in a meeting ironically, to discuss what meetings they would find most useful and how we should structure regular meetings over the month and year.

The way I started to think about meetings that I controlled and that my team controlled was through using these seven check steps, which I found helped me to limit the number of meetings and more importantly ensure that meetings were as productive as possible.

1. Objective
2. Output
3. Who
4. Communicate

5. Structure
6. Time
7. Follow up

Objective

Be clear on the purpose and objectives of the meeting. You should be able to state the purpose or objective of the meeting clearly to all attendees. For example, "The objective of this meeting is to gain agreement on the budget for 2023" or "The purpose of this meeting is to brainstorm ideas for this year's customer conference."

Output

As well as stating objectives it helps the success of a meeting if you can define and articulate your expected output or success criteria up front. By stating the expected output, you are managing your own and others' expectations. In the case of the Budget meeting example, you are looking for a final agreement. This is a significant request and worth being explicit about. In the case of the brainstorming meeting example, you are letting everyone know it is about getting to the ideas stage only and that you are not expecting the ideas to be prioritised or worked up into objectives.

For example, "The output of this meeting should be a final agreement on the budget" or "The output of this meeting should be a list of ideas to takeaway and review"

Who

This is always a tricky one. You want the right people in the room, based on need, expertise, and ability to add value. We all know there is a political dimension to think about as well which means we have to ask the question who has a vested interest in this meeting or the objective it pertains to.

To avoid having too many people in the room who are not directly relevant to a specific meeting you can think about using the RACI model (see below) to make sure the right people attend and also that you can identify who needs to be informed but does not need to be consulted (in other words do not need to attend).

Limit the number of people to those who are necessary wherever possible, but don't forget the value of naïve contributors to certain kinds of meetings to provide an alternative point of view and to challenge assumptions. Think about whether you need an external facilitator also, this could be external to your team but from within the organisation. Finally, do you need someone to take notes and produce minutes?

R	Those responsible or doing the work and completing the objective
A	The owner of the project accountable for its completion
C	Stakeholders to be consulted for expertise, input or sign off
I	Stakeholders who should be informed of project and progress

Communicate

Communication is vital in every aspect of life and work. Poor communication is often the cause of things going wrong. Even when setting meetings communication is key and is often forgotten about in the rush to get on with things.

Good communication about the purpose, expected output and why you want someone to attend can make the difference between people turning up motivated and ready to go vs. not turning up or turning up confused and annoyed that they are in a meeting, and they don't really know why!

Remember you are asking for people's valuable time, so respect their time and their priorities. Think about how you can best communicate the purpose and output of the meeting, the context of why it is important and why you would value their attendance.

For example, using the brainstorming meeting we might want to say, "We are preparing for this year's all important Customer Conference and would really value your input into making it the best yet! We are holding a brainstorming session to capture ideas for the conference and at the end of the meeting we hope to have a list of ideas to takeaway and review. Please make time to attend this session as your experience will be invaluable to help us generate innovative ideas."

The other thing to communicate is any pre-work required, in our budget approval example, because the desired outcome is final approval it may be that you need to send prereading in the form of an executive summary of the budget and any key points to note.

Structure

The structure of the meeting, including the place, people's roles and agenda is important to ensure a successful and productive outcome. Think about the appropriate setting and agenda for the type of meeting you want to run. For meetings with a defined specific purpose, regular governance, board, or an update meeting then a more tightly defined agenda is appropriate.

Defining people's role up front can also be useful if you want specific people to do certain things in the meeting, this ensures people are more prepared and you can get on with the meeting more efficiently.

Time

This is one of the most important elements, and one that is likely to cause a lot of angst if you get it wrong. Try to limit the objectives or purpose of the meeting to what is absolutely necessary. Avoid the temptation of thinking to yourself "I've got everyone together so why don't I also cover XYZ while they are trapped!".

Another thing you can do is let people go if their input is no longer required or they have finished they part of the agenda. There is nothing worse than a couple of bored disengaged people fidgeting and looking at their devices when you still have work to be done. Don't fight it, if they are no longer needed and they don't want to be there just let them go.

Keep an eye on the time all the way through the meeting, be flexible with agenda items and keep the agenda moving forward.

It may be that you drop an agenda item or that you cut one short, but the main thing is to be alert to the time and not let it get away with you. If you are intimately involved in the whole meeting, ask someone to keep track of time and to shout up when you are off track.

Follow Up

This is another forgotten element in the management of meetings, and one of the reasons they can be seen as non-productive. Let people know what the outputs of the meeting were, how they will be useful in furthering your project or helping the organisation and send an update if relevant when you have reached the next stage in the project.

This makes people feel good about using their time in your meetings, they feel valued and that they have helped accomplish something. These feelings are core to what motivates people, so use them to create meeting fans rather than meeting sceptics.

Meaningful Reporting

Reports are the other notorious time killer, the principles on how to improve the efficiency of reporting, are the same as those covered in this chapter for meetings. You can, of course, manage the level of reporting in your own team. There should be a definite need for the information, it should add value and the objective, timing and structure of the report should be clearly communicated. Think long and hard about exactly what you need and regularly check whether the information collected by reporting is being used for anything of value.

Don't let the people who love writing reports or who are overly verbose determine the content of the report. Focus on information that is useful and necessary and that serves a purpose.

Managing the report requirements from other sources is an altogether more challenging task. As a minimum you should aim to question the person requesting the information as to what they need it for and how it is used. Challenge whenever possible the reporting burden on you and your team to ensure it is reasonable and that it is being used for something valuable.

Champion and Advocate

I want to finish this principle with a word on being a champion and advocate for your team. It makes a lot of sense to champion your people and the team as a whole. This is the logical thing to do if you are an empowering leader because you believe in supporting people and you believe in building a high performing team and sharing in their success. Spending time championing your teams' abilities and success, as well as advocating for them as needed, is time well spent.

The first thing to do is present successes as the team's success not yours alone. There may be occasions where you get your head down and really drive a project or negotiate a deal and then sure take the glory, but generally your glory comes from representing the team.

Don't just champion success you can also talk about the way your team works, the way it collaborates, innovates and your team culture. Use your team members to represent at key meetings and presentations. Get them on to the agenda and let them represent you at key times, you can coach them and support them to shine and show what a good job you are doing developing your people.

The traditional model based on amassing power for the individual would not recommend doing this with your people, because of fear of them overshadowing you. This is still the case in politics, which is all about personal power and individual glory, you can make your mind up whether this approach consistently leads to high performing teams and consistent competent success!

There may be times when you need to defend and advocate for one of your team or the team as a whole. As long as you are confident the team or individual was working to the best of their abilities and with the right motives, and within the ethical and governance norms of the organisation you should be willing to stand your ground for them in the spirit of high emotional safety and learning from mistakes and failures, as well as successes.

It is best to analyse the situation before acting and gather the facts. Make sure you understand what happened, speak to those involved and make an assessment. If it is something that has gone beyond the ethical or governance rules of the company, then you need to ensure you handle it through the correct HR or legal channels.

You need to take a balanced approach to ensure that you are not showing any favouritism and that you are acknowledging where lessons should be learned. Ensure that you defend your team or people appropriately and acknowledge where things have gone wrong and be ready to explain how you are going to take on the learnings and move forward.

You want to protect your relationships internally so use sensitive but assertive communication, remaining professional and using objective specific language to explain your position. Using the techniques of Non-Violent Communication (NVC) outlined in Chapter 9 will help you do this in a way that reduces the chance of an aggressive or defensive reaction from the other party. Use the principles of NVC to get the observed, detailed, and specific information you need from the other party to ensure that the criticism is based on specific observed behaviour. Remember the coaching fundamentals covered in Chapter 8, listen, reflect, and question so that you can fully understand the issues, and respond to it correctly and calmly with all the available information.

Your Objectives and Actions from this Chapter

- Recognise your role in providing resources, protecting, and championing your team
- Use the time freed up from having a high performing self-managed team to build a network and secure resources
- Protect the team from excess pressure, interference, and time wasters
- Use best practices in managing meetings and reports
- Manage change consciously and with empathy
- Champion the team whenever you can and fight their corner when you need to

11. In Conclusion

"Before you are a leader, success is all
about growing yourself. When you become
a leader, success is all about
growing others."

Jack Welch

I wrote this book to help people in leadership roles because I believe getting the most out of your people is the key to sustainable business performance and that leadership behaviours are critical to building a high-performance culture.

Through many years of success and failure, trial and error, observation, and study I believe that all leaders need support to find their best self and be able to bring out the best in their people. I became a coach to help leaders become self-aware, to enable them to communicate their vision, build a shared purpose and to create highly effective teams.

I hope this book can help you to develop your team through your leadership.

The 7 key principles of leadership covered in this book; I believe give you a straightforward, useful guide to make changes that you can implement in the workplace to make a real difference.

As I said in the introduction, like everything in life that delivers real value and satisfaction becoming an Empowering Leader takes effort, commitment, and bravery.

Holding a mirror up to yourself and recognising that you may need to change some of your behaviours is big step for many.

Being open to feedback, being willing to be wrong, to admit you don't know everything takes courage and fortitude. Those who strive to achieve high levels of self-awareness and openness are those who are indeed described as "natural leaders" that people listen to and respect.

Building a shared purpose with your team is so fundamental to building effective, high-performing teams that if you don't do it, you are much less likely to be successful in the long term. If you don't have a shared purpose, you are not a team you are a group of individuals and as we saw with Google's research individual performance does not correlate to team performance.

Having a clear direction and being able to be decisive when the time comes are critical leadership traits that cannot be forgotten whilst building an inclusive, creative, and open culture. You still have to lead. And a key part of leadership is giving direction and making the final call.

Delegating effectively is such a fundamental part of good leadership that without doing it well, in my view, you will struggle to fulfil your true potential successful as a leader. Strive to become an Empowering leader. Whenever possible give people the space to be their best self and do their best work by delegating effectively and empowering them to succeed. But remember empowerment must be accompanied by the resources, support and relationship that actively enables people to be truly empowered.

Coaching is the magic that allows you to maximise people's potential, to grow their confidence in themselves and to build engagement. Using coaching techniques as a leader supports everything we are trying to achieve using the Empowering

Leadership model. It provides a framework for better communication and better relationships.

Creating an environment with high levels of emotional or psychological safety is central to the team becoming a learning team, which is what the Google research and other studies have determined is the key ingredient to high performance in a team. Learning together through sharing success, fails and things that didn't go to plan, means increased creativity, innovation, and competition beating performance.

When you have built your self-managed, high performing team you will have freed up your time by getting out of their way and allowing them to do their job. You can use that time to concentrate on strategic development and to further enable your team's success, and therefore your success. By protecting them from unnecessary pressure and stress, providing the resources they need and championing them internally and externally.

You may be thinking that you need some support and help to make progress in some areas described in this book, which is a feeling many will have. Help is out there. Find a good coach or mentor who can support you through the journey and speed up the process.

Step by Step

The first step is to complete an audit of where you are as a leader and where your team is at. Ask the team for their honest input, thoughts, and ideas as well as seeking input from peers, customers and other stakeholders. Seek feedback and input from the team regularly to build the trust in them that you are listening and are open. Make a prioritised plan of what you want to work on and take it step by step. One of the oldest cliches is "Rome wasn't built in a day", and we know there is no such thing as an overnight success. But do make sure to communicate your intentions to your team at the beginning of your journey, involve them from the start and use that as the first step in opening up and building a closer relationship built on trust.

Thank You

Thanks for taking the time and investing in this book. I would love to hear your feedback and would be happy to answer any questions you may have. So, get in touch via my website www.owleadershipcoaching.com. I look forward to the conversation!

Good luck in your life and career, I hope you find the joy in helping people and your team develop, grow, and perform to their maximum potential.

Bibliography

Whitmore, J. (2017). Coaching for Performance. 5th ed, Nicholas Brealey Publishing.

Edmondson, A.C. (2018) The Fearless Organization: Creating Psychological Safety in the Workplace for Learning, Innovation, and Growth. Wiley Publishing.

Rosenberg M.B. PHD (2015). NonViolent Communication, a Language of Life - Changing Tools for Healthy Relationships, Puddle Dancer Press (US); 3rd ed.

Schein E.H. and Schein P.A. (2018). Humble Leadership. Berrett-Koehler Publishers; Illustrated ed.

Lawrence-Wilkes, L., and Ashmore, L., (2014) The Reflective Practitioner in Professional Education, Palgrave Macmillan.

Dweck, C. (2006). Mindset: The New Psychology of Success. Ballantine Books

Clutterbuck D, (2020) Coaching the Team at Work 2: The definitive guide to team coaching, Nicholas Brealey International; 4th ed.

Evidence for a Collective Intelligence Factor in the Performance of Human Groups. Anita Williams Woolley et al., 686 (2010); Science 330, DOI: 10.1126/science.1193147

Managing Yourself: The Boss as Human Shield https://hbr.org/2010/09/managing-yourself-the-boss-as-human-shield, by R.I. Sutton (2010)

Psychological Safety is the Secret to Workplace Success (2019) https://www.uab.edu/reporter/resources/learning-development/item/8770-psychological-safety-is-the-secret-to-workplace-success

The Future of Work https://www.mckinsey.com/featured-insights/future-of-work McKinsey (2022)

Kline. N (1999). Time to Think: Listening to Ignite the Human Mind. Cassell

Hirsch J. (2017) The Feedback Fix: Dump the Past, Embrace the Future, and Lead the Way to Change Rowman and Littlefield Publishers

Collaborative Overload https://hbr.org/2016/01/collaborative-overload by R. Cross, R. Rebele, A. Grant (2016)

What Google Learned From Its Quest to Build the Perfect Team https://www.nytimes.com/2016/02/28/magazine/what-google-learned-from-its-quest-to-build-the-perfect-team.html. by C. Duhigg (2016)

Hood et al (2016). Mediating effects of psychological safety in the relationship between team affectivity and transactive memory systems. Journal of Organisational Behaviour, Wiley

Psychological safety and the critical role of leadership development, survey (2021) https://www.mckinsey.com/capabilities/people-and-organizational-performance/our-insights/psychological-safety-and-the-critical-role-of-leadership-development

This Is What Leadership Will Be In 2030 (forbes.com) https://hbr.org/2022/08/quiet-quitting-is-about-bad-bosses-not-bad-employees by Jack Zenger and Joseph Folkman

D. Goleman et al. (2018), Self-Awareness (HBR Emotional Intelligence Series). Harvard Business Review

How to Incorporate Realistic Optimism Into Your Life (2021) https://www.forbes.com/sites/forbescoachescouncil/2021/01/07/how-to-incorporate-realistic-optimism-into-your-life/?sh=31306c2476f0

The future of leadership: anticipating 2030 https://www. grantthornton.global/en/insights/articles/leadership-2030/

Simerson B.K. (2011). Strategic Planning: A Practical Guide to Strategy Formulation and Execution. Praeger (Kindle Edition)